ALL

HEALING

IS

THROUGH

GOD

MY CLARIFICATION OF . . . A COURSE IN MIRACLES
BY SAUL STEINBERG
The Original Printer Of A Course In Miracles

Mind and Miracles
16363 Cammi Lane
Fort Lauderdale, Florida 33326

Printed in:
The United States of America
by:
Mind and Miracles
16363 Cammi Lane
Fort Lauderdale, Florida 33326
305-389-8076
Order Toll Free
800-SAL-VATN

2nd Printing December, 1993

Dedication

This book is dedicated to my cousin, my teacher,
my brother, my friend . . .
Paul J. Steinberg

If there is one man we can truly say is responsible,
for group activity, for seeing the need to help others,
with clarification of the Course, it is Paul.

Paul saw the need in the very beginning,
and in the mid 1970's,
became one of the first teachers of the Course,
and gave himself, unceasingly.

Paul is gone in body but most definitely not in Spirit.

So many of us in the Course
remember him and love him.

*You . . . are a beautiful child
of a Loving Mother/Father GOD,
In whom He/She is well pleased.*

ALL HEALING IS THROUGH GOD

Table Of Contents

Table Of Contents

FOREWORD

It is quite possible and probably true, that *A Course In Miracles* has reached more people, since it's official publishing in June of 1976, than Jesus reached in his entire Ministry, some 2000 years ago. The Course is now in every country in this world and as I travel throughout this country, it seems that every town, city and state, has a miracle group, or at least someone studying the Course. On TV, I hear people using language, sometimes line for line, from the Course and there are thousands of books, trying to explain the Course. I have often thought how wonderful it would be, if we had a written account covering Jesus' Ministry, written and compiled during the time he walked this planet and tried to get his Wisdom heard and believed. As far as I know, this never truly happened and my guess is that a good deal of what we are told he said and did, came after he decided to leave his body.

I'm certain that *A Course In Miracles* came and was given to us at the time that it did, because we were and are ready for it, and that it could be taken down, recorded, typed, printed and published and presented to the world accurately, word for word, just as it was given. As a matter of fact, I had heard early into my participation of printing the Course, that Jesus said "this time .... there will be no mistakes", meaning of course, that the interpretation of his message cannot be misconstrued, misinterpreted, or confused It is crystal clear, what he is saying and it is my belief, that the message of today is exactly the very same message of two thousand years ago. That is why I am putting it down on paper while I'm here, and no one will have to hear or read someone elses account of The Printing Of A Course In Miracles.

The Printing Of A Course In Miracles

In 1975 my life seemed to be pretty much set in doing what I had been born to do. I had chosen to learn the printing trade, starting at the tender age of twelve and one half and by this time I was in business for myself with my own printing and advertising business. Contrary to what has been written before, I was not consciously seeing, looking for, or in any way searching for anything like A Course In Miracles or any other Spiritual/Psychological 'how to' study. The only 'how to' that I was interested in was how to make a living for myself, my wife and my three children. So it was a great surprise to me, this whole assignment of setting every line of type, assembling the three books that have captivated the imagination and thinking of the world and to be sure, has changed the lives of myself, my family and everyone else that is guided into my life.

The story of The Printing Of The Course In Miracles really must start about twenty years or so before I actually printed the Course, when my wife Judy and I were invited to my cousin Paul's new home in White Plains, New York. Paul had recently married his wife Roberta and Judy and I were also newly weds. Since we had never met Roberta and Paul and Roberta had never met Judy, Paul planned a small gathering on a Saturday night and since we lived in Yonkers, New York at the time, we accepted his invitation and were indeed looking forward to it. Paul earned his living in a liquor store and was in business with his mother Roy and in anticipation of the gala evening he was planning, he had not only brought home every conceivable wine known to man and woman, but also took the time to learn the pronunciation of all these foreign vintages and also researched what kind of grapes, created the wine and what years were the best years for that particular wine.

After taking our coats, Paul made the introductions, there was one other couple there that evening, and he immediately started offering the different wines and giving their history and pedigrees as well. I remember his approaching Judy and saying, 'this is such and such wine from the Loire Valley in France, the grape is and he would describe the grape in exquisite detail and after a two to three minute explanation, he then asked Judy if she would care for some'.

Judy politely said, no thank you. Then he started with 'this is such and such wine from Germany, the grape is' and he would again go into great detail and again Judy would reply, no thank you. Paul went through his entire repertoire of wines, he covered the entire planet it seemed and after each detailed explanation, Judy would politely say once again, 'no thank you'. Finally having reached the end of his stock of wines and also his prepared mini lectures on every wine he had brought home in desperation. Paul finally asked Judy, 'well what kind of wine would you like?' . . . without any delay or confusion, Judy replied, 'do you happen to have any Manischewitz'? Paul looked at Judy, smiled and said 'nope, sorry that's the one wine I didn't bring home, or research'. Judy settled for a diet coke. After about an hour or so of sharing different stories and talking about our experiences as kids growing up in the Bronx, the Boy Scouts and Troop 113, Monroe High School, etc., Paul stood up and made an announcement. He said, that he was going to dim the lights, as we were about to see some movies. I looked around the room for a movie projector and screen, but saw neither. I thought for a moment that perhaps both were hidden behind an artificial wall, Hollywood style, but that was not the case. Paul asked Judy and I to sit on a couch facing a blank white wall, along with the other couple present and Paul sat to the right of us on a club chair, with Roberta sitting to the left us on another club chair. Dramatically, he said, 'now fix your attention to the wall in front of you'. I asked 'what are we supposed to be seeing'? He replied 'just watch the wall in front of you, don't take your eyes off of the wall.' I was starting to feel Judy's discomfort, but I was still trying to fix my attention to the blank wall in front of me. Suddenly Paul very excitedly, yelled 'do you see him'? I asked 'do I see who'? Paul said once again, 'don't you see him'? Once again, I asked 'don't I see who'? Paul said 'it's Jesus'. I asked, 'who?' Paul repeated . . . 'It's Jesus'. Judy, now really feeling quite uncomfortable, gave me her elbow in my ribs and through the corner of her mouth, whispered, 'let's get out of here, this guy is crazy'. I whispered back, just relax, we just got here. Paul once again asked 'don't you see him, it's Jesus of Nazareth? Suddenly the couple sitting next to us on the couch cried out, 'yes we see him, we see him'. Judy gave me another elbow in the ribs and once again through the corner of her mouth, in a slightly louder whisper said 'let's get out of here, this guy and the couple next to us are definitely, crazy'.

Paul now started to give us a description of what he and the other couple were seeing, he said 'Jesus was wearing a brown robe, with sandals and he was holding a staff' and the other couple said 'yes it's beautiful, he's beautiful' and with that for the third time that evening, Judy's elbow, now harder than the first two times, landed in my ribs and she now, most impatiently demanded, 'let's get out of here, right now. Paul heard Judy this time and he said 'maybe Jesus is a little too much for you at this time, let me bring in someone else for both of you'. I said, 'come on Paul, do you expect us to believe that we've just been paid a visit by Jesus and now that we couldn't see him, you're going to invite someone else to your apartment, here in White Plains'? Paul smiled and said 'but of course' I asked 'who this time'? Paul answered, 'how about Alexander The Great'? Judy this time very much annoyed and wanting to leave, said, 'if you don't take me home, I'm going by myself'. I said, 'let's see if we can see and meet Alexander The Great, perhaps Jesus was a bit too intense for us'. Once again the lights were dimmed and Paul asked everyone to focus on the blank white wall in front of us for Alexander's arrival. Again the couple next to us exclaimed 'it's him, it's Alexander'. This time Judy got up from the couch and said in a most angry, agitated tone, I'm leaving, with you or without you. Since she didn't drive at that time, I got up, excusing ourselves with the flimsy excuse that I had a busy day tomorrow and we left Paul and Roberta's home that evening. The fact of the matter is . . . Judy and I fled in terror.

The story now shifts to 1975, some twenty years later, Judy and I now live in a town called Deer Park, on Long Island in New York, have three teen aged kids, Paul, Linda, and Sandi and I have now been in business in a place called Farmingdale, Long Island, New York for four years, in a combination printing and advertising business, which has been going quite well. I had heard that Paul had recently moved to Long Island, along with Roberta and their three children and was now in the swimming pool business, but in all of the years in between, there had been little or had no contact between Paul and myself, since that night we fled in terror. One day the telephone rang and I once again heard Paul's voice and he said Hi ya Spank, (he and others had called me Spanky, since as a child many people thought I resembled Spanky of the Our Gang comedies, and many folks think I still do) and he continued, it's been a long time. I agreed and asked him what was new in his life, about his family, business and some other things, when he abruptly stopped the conversation and said, 'Spank, I need a favor'. 'What kind of favor', I asked? He started to tell me about a new business venture in which he and his sister's husband Irv German, were involved dealing with something I had never heard of before, called Parapsychology and that they had assembled the world's leading Parapsychologists into a group and that the world was eagerly awaiting the materials that all of these respected and learned Parapsychologists were ready to give to the world. Paul then started to tell me about a Newsletter they were trying to put together and he said that he knew that I had had a great deal of experience in the putting together of Newsletters and asked if I would be interested in getting involved. I asked him, 'are you offering me a job? He replied, 'well in a way' . . . I interrupted, 'how much does it pay'? He hesitated and said 'well . . . it really doesn't pay anything, but the experience would be invaluable for you and it could lead to many other wonderful things'. I quickly replied, 'not interested, I have all the work I can handle and more experience is not something I am in any great need of at this moment'. Seeing that the experience and the many other wonderful things weren't working, Paul then used a different tactic . . . begging. His beg was, 'come on Spank, I really do need your help and for us difficult, for you easy', etc. He then used the one line that he knew would get to me, he said, 'how about for old times sake'. I hesitated and before I could turn him down again, he said, 'I'll be over in a half hour . . . where the hell is your office'? I gave him directions to the Huntington Quadrangle and a half hour later, he was standing in front of me.

He did something he had never done before, he took me around, gave me a great big bear hug and I noticed he was clutching a large sign like object and I asked, what's that? He said that it was a business plan that he was given, but he didn't elaborate. I asked could I see it and he handed this large chart to me and what I saw was something that looked like an electric schematic, with two boxes on top, branching into four boxes, branching into eight boxes, ultimately branching into sixteen boxes. The top two boxes showed Newsletter in one box and Publishing in the box next to it. The other boxes also contained the game plan for his up and coming venture and I was astounded at the completeness of the work he had done. I asked again if he had help in putting this whole business plan together and he said, yes and let it go at that. He explained that the reason the Newsletter wasn't coming together was that all of the Parapsychologists wanted to see their writings and articles up front and no one wanted their articles at the end of the Newsletter. He then asked me a loaded question, that if I were him, what would I do to get my Newsletter printed and published. I replied, 'if I were you, I'd get someone like me to do it for you'. Without giving me a chance to refuse again, he said, 'you're hired'. Just what I needed, a job, with no pay. I said 'what now'? and Paul said call Judy and tell her you will be home late this evening. I called Judy and told her that I was going into Manhattan and her first question was 'what for?' and I told her I was attending a meeting of Parapsychologists her next question was what's a Parapsychologist? I said, I'm not sure, I guess, some kind of a scientist. Her next question was, with who? When I answered Paul Steinberg, she probably remembered back to our experience in White Plains, some twenty years earlier and asked, 'will I ever see you again'?

About an hour later Paul and I were sitting in Paul's Buick station wagon in the parking lot of the Huntington Quadrangle waiting for Paul's brother in law, my cousin, Irv German. Irv drove up, got into the back seat of the wagon and we were off to our meeting. It was a short drive from the quadrangle to the Long Island Expressway and as Paul headed the Buick west towards New York City I wondered what I was doing on the L.I.E. instead of being home, eating a good dinner.

Something was wrong, real wrong. We had been driving on the Long Island Expressway for about fifteen minutes, in the height of rush hour and Paul was doing sixty five miles an hour, without one slow down or stop. This wasn't right. I looked around, on the sides, in back, in front, there was no traffic. Paul watching me looking around asked 'something wrong Spank'? I answered, yes, there's no traffic, very, very unusual for this time of evening. Paul just smiled as he continued heading for Manhattan. We went another fifteen miles and I couldn't believe that we had not been forced to stop, not even once. Again Paul saw me looking around and I asked, 'Paul hake you ever seen traffic this light during rush hour on the L.I.E.'? He answered, I'm never bothered with traffic on any road, I'm ever on. I looked at him and asked, 'how come'? Paul's answer was a startling one, he replied that Abdulla had cleared the Expressway of all traffic for us. We were experiencing a very rare happening on the Long Island Expressway, we were zooming along at sixty five miles an hour, with no traffic, no delays, not even a slow down and Paul is telling me it's due to Abdulla. I looked around again and I asked, 'who's Abdulla'? He replied, 'Abdulla is my Genie who helps me with everything I need, whenever I'm in need of help. I knew from my experience some twenty years earlier in White Plains, that my cousin wasn't playing with a full deck and now he's saying he has a Genie, that does his bidding. I had no idea, that he was this far gone. Paul then volunteered that all he needed to do was to ask Abdulla's help and it would always arrive, soon after the request was made. My next question was, 'how could a nice Jewish boy from the Bronx, have an Arab Genie''? Paul replied immediately, 'Abdulla has no prejudices and neither do I'. He continued, 'no task, no requests, no help, is ever rejected by Abdulla, as long as it is helpful to all involved. Crazy as a loon, I thought, but here we were speeding down the L.I.E. at sixty five miles an hour.

As we continued on our journey into New York City, the one crazy thing that was occurring, was that there was no traffic, obstructions or delays slowing us down, or in our path. When we got to the city line and entered Queens, I looked at Paul, he sensed my question, and blurted out, that's right Abdulla. The trip from my office into Manhattan, a distance of thirty nine miles is normally a two to two and one half hour trip in rush hour traffic. We had left my office in Melville, at ten minutes after five and a half hour later we were in Queens getting ready to go over the fifty-ninth street bridge. The ride over the bridge is normally in traffic a twenty five to thirty minute crossing and that evening we sped across in five minutes. Again I looked at Paul and once again he smiled and said 'that's right, Abdulla'. The amazing journey continued, driving uptown on third avenue, then through Central Park onto Central Park West and Paul made a left turn into eighty ninth street and I asked, 'how about parking'? 'No problem for Abdulla', Paul replied. Sure enough, after going not more than a one third of a city block, a car pulled out of a spot and Paul backed the big brown Buick station wagon in and we were parked. Easiest parking I had ever seen in Manhattan . . . fastest trip from Long Island to Manhattan, I had ever experienced.

We took the elevator up to our meeting. As we entered the Parapsychologist's meeting I noticed that there were about thirty or thirty five men and women discussing some of the new things they were working on and Paul introduced me to everyone as his cousin, who knew everything there was to know about putting a Newsletter together, but knew nothing at all about Parapsychology. The game plan that came together that evening was, since the problem seemed to be that everyone wanted their article to be the lead off article, since I knew absolutely nothing about Parapsychology, I would read all of the articles submitted, pick out the most interesting sounding articles and proceed with putting together the Newsletter. Everyone seemed to agree that it sounded like a good way to proceed and when we left that night, I had a briefcase full of articles and I had promised to come back the following week with all of the articles typeset, a new and appropriate logo design for the Newsletter and the best darn publication, ever done.

Paul, Irv, and I drove back to Long Island and as we each got into our cars, I knew I had my work cut out for me. As I started to read the materials the next morning, I thought to myself, that these materials were or seemed to be right out of Twilight Zone. During the next few days I designed a logo and masthead, set all the type, arranged the articles in an order, which I felt was the proper rotation and even printed up a hundred copies in two colors, to give out at the next meeting. I felt I had really done a fantastic job, for a guy who knew absolutely nothing about Parapsychology and I truly believed that everyone was going to love 'my' Newsletter.

On Tuesday, the day we were to have our second meeting and I was going to present my creation to the group of Parapsychologists, I received a call from Paul, telling me that we had to go into New York City a little earlier and could I be ready to leave my office by three thirty that afternoon. Since I had the Newsletter all set to go, I told him that I didn't think it would be a problem but asked why, since our meeting wasn't till seven thirty. He replied that he was giving a lecture at his son's high school the following day and needed to pick up a film from a woman who had borrowed the film from the doctor who had made the film. Foolishly, I inquired, 'what kind of film'? He answered very casually, oh, the film is about a Brazilian peasant man, living in the jungles of South America. This peasant man performs operations, all day long and the people that go to this man are Healed instantly and what is really amazing about this man, is that this uneducated Brazilian peasant has never had any education, medical training or schooling of any description and . . . uses no instruments to perform these operations, but relies only on a penknife. Paul went on to say that this peasant man had become so well known in South America, that even the President of Brazil had gone to this man deep in the Brazilian jungle and had asked for and received Healing. My first thought at that moment was that my cousin had really flipped completely and was not playing with a full deck. I asked him what that had to do with going into New York earlier and again he replied that the Doctor who had made this film, and had also written a book about his observing this phenomenon had lent the film to a woman who lived on eighty first street and Central Park West and while he had never met this woman, Paul had heard about her and was anxious to meet her as he had heard that she was very much involved with Parapsychology and he thought that she might just have an interest in joining in with Paul's group of Parapsychologists. He then asked me if I would drive that afternoon and when I looked out of the window and saw the rain coming down rather heavily, I quickly replied, no sir. He then said something real strange, which once again I had never heard him or anyone else say, he said, 'but Spank, my Guides have asked me to tell you that not only should you drive today but also that you and Irv should accompany me up to this woman's apartment, so you can meet this lady. I said no way told and Paul to be at my office at three thirty and went back to work.

Paul got to my office at three fifteen and gave me another one of his bear hugs and said . . my guides still insist that you are to drive and that both Irv and you are supposed to go up to this gal's apartment to pick up the Arrigo film. I looked at Paul and asked. . . . what are these Guides you keep talking about, the only Guides I knew about were the Guides that you would encounter on or during a sight seeing trip. Paul then explained to me that Guides were like Angels, who were always there to aid, assist and help and that his Guides had requested that Irv, Paul and I were to go up to this woman's apartment to pick up the film and that I was to drive into Manhattan that afternoon. Once again I found myself hearing the theme of Twilight Zone in my head and I knew . . . this time I really knew, that my cousin Paul had truly flipped out.

I once again looked out of the window saw the rain coming down even harder than I had seen it that morning and told Paul that I had on a brand new suit and that no way did I want to ruin the suit or even meet this mystery lady. Paul was insistent and finally got his way and the three of us were back on The Long Island Expressway on our way to eighty first street and Central Park West, the rain still coming down like a typhoon.

Something was once again wrong, very wrong, very, very wrong. Here was Irv, Paul and I driving west on the L.I.E. and I was actually flying along at sixty five miles an hour, in the rain no less, on what was considered by most who had ever been on it . . . the longest parking lot in the world. I looked at Paul and he looked back at me knowing my question before I asked it and he replied yes that's right, Abdulla. As we crossed the fifty ninth street bridge once again and were crossing without even one stop he looked at me and said, 'all you have to do is ask'. As I was driving through Central Park, Paul asked me, 'what would it take for you to come up with me and pick up the film. I replied number one, you or your Abdulla would have to stop this rain, so my suit wouldn't get ruined and number two you or Abdulla would really have to do the impossible and find us a parking spot on Eighty first street and Central Park West. Paul without a moments hesitation replied, 'no problem, done'. As I came out of Central Park and made my right turn towards eighty first street, I saw an amazing thing occur. I saw a car, actually leaving a parking place diagonally across the street from the building where this lady lived. Now you have to understand the significance of this 'happening', that anyone living and owning a car in Manhattan, where the city officials have invented a cruel type of torture called alternate side of the street parking, people when buying a new car or used, generally at least once are able to find a parking space by waking up at three a.m., going downstairs and moving said car, so that they won't be towed away and in general, park that car in those two valued parking places and never for the entire life of owning said car, move it at all, until such time as they decide to sell it. Here was a spot being provided for us, a miracle, an absolute miracle. Paul said 'Ok Spank, there's your spot. The rain was still falling quite hard and I said to Paul, 'what about all this rain'? Paul replied 'you and Irv need only to get out of the car with me and I promise both of you, that you positively will not get wet. More Twilight Zone. The three of us got out of the car without umbrellas and amazingly, not one of us got a single drop of water on ourselves. It was like an invisible umbrella was protecting us from the rain and as we crossed the street, to the building on the corner of eighty first street and Central Park West . . . the only thought I could think was . . weird . . . very weird.

The three of us walked into the building on the corner and we were greeted by a doorman whose function it was to screen and announce all visitors and I heard Paul say to him, tell Mrs. Skutch that Mr. Steinberg is here to pick up the film. Not a word about Irv or myself, just Mr. Steinberg. The doorman made the announcement over the intercom and I very distinctly heard the voice on the other end of the intercom say, 'send them up'. I wondered how this woman could possibly know that we were going to go up to her apartment, when Irv and I had no idea that we would.

We entered the self service elevator, Irv, Paul and I and when we got to the fifth floor, the elevator door slid open and standing there was a beautiful dark haired lady standing at the entrance to the apartment and her first words to us were . . 'good evening gentlemen, I'm Judy Skutch and I was expecting you, you are numbers seven, eight and nine'. More Twilight Zone, I thought. I asked her what that statement meant and she replied that she had had a vision that morning that she would be visited that day by ten people and that number seven would be a teacher of GOD, number eight would be a printer and number nine would be a business man. As I listened to her, I knew immediately that I most certainly was the printer, I also knew that Irv was without a doubt the businessman, but for the life of me, I couldn't begin to imagine who she was talking about, as a teacher of GOD. Judy took our coats, hung them up in the hall closet and ushered the three of us into a small study to the right of the foyer. In the room as I remember it, was a couch, two chairs and a large chest of drawers, filled with books on the top shelves and three large pull out drawers, on the bottom. She asked Irv and I to sit on the couch and she asked Paul to sit on the chair facing the other chair in the room, in which she promptly sat down and all of us were now seated. She looked deeply into Paul's eyes and then asked the most embarrassing question I had ever heard asked of a Jewish person. The question was . . .

'What Is Your Opinion of Jesus?'

Both Irv and I became extremely uncomfortable and I could actually feel the hair on the back of my neck standing on end and at that moment I felt more discomfort, than I had ever felt for Paul. Paul never broke his stare from Judy's eyes and in a quiet subdued voice replied . . .

'Oh, you mean the Master J, He Is Without A Doubt . .
The Greatest Teacher, The World Has Ever Known.'

I stared straight at my cousin and my thoughts were, where did he get that from? Judy's eyes and Paul's eyes, never broke contact and with Paul's answer, Judy wheeled around, pulled the bottom drawer forward and pulled out what appeared to be a printer's gray box of papers. After taking the box out of the drawer, she placed the box on Paul's knees and said . . .

'You . . . Are To Have This!'

Paul . . as if he somehow knew, what was contained in the box, replied, thank you and with that, Judy got up and said, please excuse me gentlemen, I'm very tired and I must get some rest. She then handed us our coats, escorted us a few feet to the elevator, the elevator door opened and she pushed the down button. The entire visit had not taken more than about twenty minutes and the last expression I noticed on Judy's lovely face seemed to be saying to me, mission accomplished.

As we were riding down in the elevator, Paul seemed to be tingling with excitement. He asked Irv and I, if we had any idea what was in this gray box of paper, that he seemed to be clutching and holding on to, so carefully. I replied jokingly, that it looked like a gray box of paper, holding about fifteen hundred sheets, from the size of the box. Irv then surprised me very much by stating that he had had a very peculiar experience while in Judy's study, when he said that he had heard and experienced a kind of high pitched whistling noise or sound, all of the time in Judy's study. Paul immediately remarked, that indeed, there were 'others' in the room with us. Irv asked Paul, 'what kind of others'? Paul replied, that there had been several Spirit Guides present, watching over the transference of 'the materials' from one Teacher Of GOD, to another Teacher Of GOD, and that he also had heard and been aware of the immense Energy and high pitched whistling sound, that Irv had experienced, in that High Powered twenty minutes. Listening to this conversation, I was fairly certain that I now had two crazy cousins and I started singing the lead into the most popular science fiction show of that time . . . Twilight Zone . . . da da da da . . . da da da da . . . da da da da, etc.

Paul looking quite serious, then told Irv and I that this material just handed to him by Judy Skutch, was some highly secret materials entitled 'A Course In Miracles' and that he had heard of it's existence, on a secret tape that had been sent to Paul, by a friend of his, by the name of Douglas Dean. According to Paul, Douglas Dean had stated on this tape that this material that Paul was now holding in his hands, was indeed some of the 'highest' Spiritual Materials ever given to us and was being called 'A Course In Miracles' and were supposed to be revealing the secrets of living and life itself. Paul then said that some of the people who had seen this Course, were referring to it as the 'Third Testament'. I couldn't restrain myself any longer and said, I haven't yet read the first two Testaments and now we have a third, come on, give me a break, let's get these Newsletters into the hands of all our Parapsychologists. With that, we got into my car, drove the short distance to eighty ninth street, made our left turn and guess what? A man pulled out of a parking place, right in front of the building, we were going to.

As we were going up to our meeting, I figured that both of my cousins had now flipped their lids but I was very excited about the work I had done and was about to present to the group of

Parapsychologists. I believed they were waiting with baited breath, for this presentation, that I had just spent a full week in preparing. As we entered the apartment, I could feel the excitement and the anticipation with all of those in the room as the moment had now come, that their long awaited publicity vehicle had finally come. Everyone was seated and I passed out the Newsletters and everyones attention was focused on their own stories, the placement of their stories and after a few minutes, there was a silence, that was to me rather deafening. I broke the silence by asking, 'how do you like it'? Nobody answered. A few seconds later, I tried again, 'does anyone like what I've done'? . . . more silence.

Paul, Irv and I left the meeting that night, and none of us knew, that it was to be the last Parapsychology meeting, any of us would ever attend, again, it was just a means that some kind of Higher Power had used to introduce the three of us to this woman we had met earlier that evening, named Judy Skutch, a lady that would change our lives very, very much, from that moment on.

As I dropped Paul and Irv off at the Huntington Quadrangle that night, Paul still very much on cloud nine, announced to Irv and I, that he was going to lock himself in his bedroom and not come out, until he had read the entire manuscript, which I estimated contained about fifteen hundred pages. I took another look at the gray box Paul was clutching and remarked . . . I'll see you in about six months. It didn't take six months, at the end of that same week, I received a call from Paul, saying that he had just finished going over the manuscript and he said that the materials were even more fantastic than he could believe and indeed it was just what he had been searching for, all of his life. He asked if he could come over to make copies of the entire manuscript on my zerox machine and quick as lightning I started to compute in my head what fifteen hundred pages times twenty five cents would come out to and I figured that Paul Steinberg would supply my profits for that day. Paul asked if he could come right over and start immediately and when I went to answer I heard myself answering in a voice not sounding like my own, 'yes come right over' and . . . 'the copies are on the house'. I looked around to see who had said that, as I knew that I had never made such a statement or offer of free copies. Paul appeared at my printing facility within a half hour, gray box with manuscript in hand and after showing him how to use the machine, he started making his copies. After about three hours, I walked over to Paul who was steadfastedly making his copies and I picked up one copy, looked at it, tried to decipher what it was saying and made a discovery, the discovery was that it seemed to be written in English, but on trying to understand what it was saying, I didn't understand any part of the page I was looking at. I couldn't imagine, what these words were trying to convey.

Paul looked up at me and saw the confusion on my face and asked me if I understood anything that I had just read? I replied, not a word, what is this stuff anyway? He looked at me, smiled and said . . . perhaps someday you will understand it. He continued making his copies and I continued with my work.

It was almost six o'clock and I wanted to call it a day and once again I walked over to Paul, picked up another copy, looked at it, tried to decipher what that page was trying to say, couldn't and put the copy back on to the large pile of copies. Paul smiled once again and said, 'Spank, this material will become the world's most important material, in time to come'. I thought to myself this cousin of mine is really off the wall and I asked him if he was almost done, as I was getting hungry. He said he was finished and he asked how much he owed me. I replied, cringing at my generosity, that I had told him the copies were on the house and that, there would be no charge. I added that the next time he needed to make copies, he should go elsewhere and use someone elses copying machine, paper and toner. He walked towards me and I could see the appreciation and love in his eyes and he said 'I love you Spank', threw his arms around me in another of his great big bear hugs and said 'I'll see you soon'. I thought to myself, yes, probably in a mental ward somewhere.

It was about two weeks later, a Sunday morning, my wife Judy and I were sitting around after reading the Sunday papers, I decided to tease Judy by asking, if she would like to take a ride over to see Paul Steinberg. I figured she would quickly refuse, remembering the frightening evening in White Plains, many years ago, but she surprised me by replying, 'sure, why not'? I was shocked, but I went to the phone anyway, dialed Paul's number and before I had a chance to say anything, I heard Paul say, 'hi Spank, what time will you be over? I asked him how he knew it was me and how did he know that we wanted to come over? He replied, 'Abdulla' I asked him for directions, he gave them to me and reminded me not to forget the cake. Judy and I stopped at the bakery and like in a Woody Allen movie, started out for Paul's home, with the white box, chocolate cake inside, tied with the red and white string. About an hour later, sitting around Paul's kitchen table, the conversation was centered around our experiences of growing up in the Bronx, and all of the great times, we had shared, as kids. Suddenly, the telephone rang, Paul got up and started talking, while Judy, Roberta and I, kept chattering away. About five minutes after Paul had answered the phone, he called out my name and said, 'Spank, it's for you'. I replied, 'it can't be, no one knew I would be here, not my children, not my friends, not even me'. He repeated, 'it's for you' I got up, took the phone from him and the voice on the other end, said, 'hello Saul, this is Judy Skutch, and we have been told, that you, are to be the printer of our three books, 'A Course In Miracles'. Startled by her words, I then asked, 'who told you'? She replied, Jesus and The Holy Spirit. I questioned, 'who'? She again replied, 'Jesus and The Holy Spirit' In disbelief, I asked, 'they mentioned my name'? She replied 'they did'. I next asked, 'were there any other people considered for this assignment'? Judy answered, well several people had volunteered to do the printing, at no cost to us, but Jesus and The Holy Spirit, told us that you are to be the printer. Immediately, I asked, 'oh, you want me to do this printing for nothing, is that it'? Judy answered, 'no, you will have and be given everything, you need to do the job. Not believing a word that she had said, I questioned, are you trying to tell me that you have had people actually volunteer to print these books for you, at no cost to you, but you've turned them down, because these guys, Jesus and The Holy Spirit as you call them, have said that I, Saul Steinberg, is to be the printer of your books, do I have it right? Judy replied, 'right on' My next question to Judy was, 'do you have the money, that it will cost to manufacture these books'? Judy replied, 'I'm afraid not'. I was amazed and next asked Judy, 'are you trying to tell me that you have had offers from others, that they would print these books for you at no charge, but these guys Jesus and The Holy Spirit said no, that Saul Steinberg should be the printer of your books, but you don't have the money at this time, but want to proceed anyway. Am I hearing this right?'

Again she replied, 'right on' My next question was, 'well where will the money, that it will cost to manufacture these books, come from'?. Very casually and assured, she answered, 'oh, the money will manifest itself'. I had absolutely no idea what this woman was talking about and once again to be polite, asked, 'are you telling me and wanting me to believe, that what you're saying is, 'that you have had several people volunteer to print your three books for you at no charge, for nothing, but Jesus and the Holy Spirit have said, no Saul Steinberg is supposed to print your books, with monies, that you don't have, do I have it right? Once again, Judy replied, 'right on'. The next thing that happened, was and still is, amazing to me, I heard my mouth, my voice and my tongue saying something totally out of character for me, at that time. Coming out of my mouth were the words, . . .

'I Would Be Honored, To Print Your Books.'

This was totally out of character for me. As a somewhat new business man, it was most definitely my policy to check any new clients out with Dun and Bradstreet, also to require a one third deposit of monies, before accepting any work, regardless of my relationship with the party that wanted the work done and yet I had just said to a perfect stranger, a woman I had met only once for about twenty minutes, here I was, saying that I would be honored, to do three books for her, not having the faintest idea, how many pages, what kind of binding, or even the desired quantity. What had I volunteered for? Surely, I must also be crazy. Judy didn't waste any further time, she shot back at me and said, 'oh Saul, that's wonderful, I want you and Paul to come back to my apartment this coming Tuesday and you both will get to meet the rest of the 'family'. It was then that I figured out where the money to be used for paying for the books, would be coming from, or as Judy had put it, how the money would 'manifest itself'. When Judy had mentioned the 'family', I assumed that the family was the Mafia and it occurred to me, that they had all the money, needed.

The following Tuesday morning, Paul and I once again got into his Buick wagon and once again we found ourselves speeding down the Long Island Expressway on our way to Judy Skutch's apartment.

This time however, Abdulla found us a parking space right in front of Judy's apartment building. We went in and this time heard the doorman clearly state, Mr. Paul Steinberg and Mr. Saul Steinberg are here to see Mrs. Skutch. Again over the intercom, I heard Judy's voice say, 'send them up'. For the second time, Judy met Paul and I at the elevator door and as the door opened, she took our coats, ushered us into her living room, a large room that seemed to be done completely in a light blue. The first person we were introduced to was a small gray haired lady and we were introduced to her as, Dr. Helen. Dr. Helen did not get up and both Paul and I shook her hand and moved on to the next part of the 'family', a tall good looking man who was introduced to us as Dr. Bill. Again we shook hands, Dr. Bill saying he was happy to meet us. The third person we met that morning was introduced to us as Dr. Ken, and I remember thinking to myself, that I had just met three Doctors, none of which had a last name and I thought to myself that it must have been quite difficult for anyone to find these three Doctors in a hospital. We then were introduced to the last member of the family, Bob Skutch, and the introductions were complete. This group definitely did not look or sound like the Mafia, and we were then asked to sit down and told we were now going to participate in a meditation . . . to ask whether it was so, that I was to indeed be the printer of A Course In Miracles. Once again an uncomfortable feeling started to come over me and, that I was definitely in the company of some very weird people, but nevertheless I figured I might as well go along and for the first time in my life, I found myself 'meditating'. About two minutes or so into the 'meditation', I opened one eye to check, to see if I was still on planet earth or somewhere in the Twilight Zone. No, I was definitely still on planet earth and I closed my one eye and waited for all this foolishness to be over. Two or three minutes later the 'meditation' was over and everyone in the room opened their eyes and everyone in the room with the exception of me, very excitedly agreed and were shaking their heads, that they had definitely received a green light and that there was definitely a yes to my being the 'right person' to be the printer of A course In Miracles. Once again a peculiar feeling started to come over me, but everyone seemed so joyous and convinced, that this was the way to go, I simply decided to do it.

The next thing that happened was that I was ushered over to Dr.

Helen and we started to talk about starting work, on the 'books'. Her knowledge of book manufacturing surprised me and the single most important thing to her was, that these three books, should be the finest, most perfect books, ever printed. Dr. Helen and I discussed, type faces, sizes, paper, bindings, and even color It was determined that I would submit various samples of everything discussed and that we would meet again the following Tuesday, which would give me a week to do some designs for the covers, to try several different typefaces, sizes and to get samples of different cover materials, to be considered. Dr. Helen surprised me with her knowledge, when she requested that the three books all had to be smythe sewn, which is an older, stronger way of binding or actually sewing books together. The method being, that one thirty two page section is placed on top of one another, in the proper rotation and then with a sewing machine, actually sewing all of the signatures together, rendering these books virtually impossible, in coming apart. Several hours later Paul and I were saying our good byes and as Judy was showing us to the door, she put her hand on my shoulder and said 'don't be concerned Saul, the monies that you need to do this work, will be coming to you, very soon'. Looking into her eyes . . . I knew that she was right and truthfully all concerns about how or when I was to be paid, were gone.

That week, I started on the cover designs, set type in several different typefaces, ordered samples of various cover stocks and started to hunt down whether or not there were any binderies left in country, that still did smythe sewing.

The Friday of that same week, a very strange thing occurred. As I was opening my mail, I spotted a peculiar looking envelope, which seemed to have foreign looking postage stamps and even the postmark looked different. On closer examination, I saw that this letter had been mailed from a place I had never heard of called Mazatland, Mexico. I opened the letter wondering what was contained within and to my utter amazement, there was a check inside of the envelope and what flopped out was a check in the amount of twenty thousand dollars, the largest check I had ever seen. The check was drawn on a bank in New Orleans, Louisiana, and was signed by a man who's name was totally unfamiliar to me, the signature on the check, read Reed Erickson. I thought to myself, this must be a joke, nobody I knew, sent checks to other people, who they knew nothing about or had never met, for twenty dollars, let alone twenty thousand dollars. Looking at the check once again, I took it down to the bank in the building, asked to see the president of the bank and showed him the check. I then asked him to find out for me if this check was any good or if this was some sort of gag, being played on me. Within a few minutes, he was on the phone, talking to the president of the bank in New Orleans checking out the validity of the check. On questioning the bank president in New Orleans, he learned that Reed Erickson was in the habit of issuing checks in large amounts of money and that it appeared to be in order and my bank president was informed, that the check was ok to deposit and I did.

The following Tuesday Paul and I went back to Judy's apartment for our second meeting with the 'family'. The progress I had made and Dr. Helen and everyone else really loved my cover designs, the look of the pages and just about everything else I had done. Dr. Helen selected a typeface called Palatino and commented that the size of the type was perfect. She then chose a light blue denim cover material for the covers and for the first time, I felt that she had made a poor choice. I pointed out to Dr. Helen that the light blue denim would soil quite easily and that it would also show fingerprints and in general would not be as practical, as they had told me, that these books would be used on a daily basis. Dr. Helen said that she disagreed and insisted that the light blue denim was the look she had seen in a meditation and everyone present agreed, that that was the cover material to be used. Well we were now most definitely on our way, but I still did not know of any binders in the New York area, who knew how, or did smythe sewing.

The work, the typesetting, was progressing nicely and although I was totally inexperienced in book printing and publishing, the one thing that my training in printing had me doing, was to squeeze as much on a page, as I possibly could. In my zeal to save these people I was working with, as much money as I could, I had assembled all three books with very little white space and indeed had bunched up and squeezed all of the materials together. I had left little or no space between Workbook Lessons and one day I received a call from Judy Skutch and her first words to me were 'stop the presses'. I explained to her that we were no where near the presses at that time and that no printing was done until all of the typeset and mechanical work was done. She explained to me that she had always wanted to use that phrase. I asked her what was wrong and she told me that Jesus and The Holy Spirit had communicated to Helen, that the Workbook was all wrong. I asked in what way and she told me that since the Workbook contained three hundred and sixty five lessons and it was meant to be one for each day, that it was pointed out to Helen that there needed to be adequate space left between lessons and that I'd have to redo the entire workbook. Judy could sense the anger and upset in my voice and she said, 'Saul don't be upset, you'll figure out a way to handle this and volunteered to pay me, for whatever the redo might cost. She also mentioned that I had already performed so many miracles, that she was confident that I would find, 'a better way'. Indeed I did, a few weeks later, the entire Workbook was completely redone and instead of resetting a single line, I just cut each one of the Lessons apart and restrung the entire three hundred and sixty five Lessons. One very expensive calamity . . . avoided.

The next thing that occurred with the printing of A Course In Miracles and this happened just as I was about to print, was another call from Judy and once again she repeated those three words, she said she had always wanted to use. Once again, I heard, 'stop the presses'. I asked 'what's wrong this time' and once again she replied, 'it's still all wrong'. I asked 'in what way' and she said that there were places in the typesetting, throughout the three books, where we needed to change the bold face roman type, to matching bold face italic type. I immediately answered that we couldn't do that because in that particular type face, that Dr. Helen had chosen, there was no bold face italic and that I had checked it out, when I had purchased the Palatino font. Judy as always being very loving and patient with me, said, 'come on Saul, you've created so many miracles with all of this, since we've started, I'm sure you'll come up with a way. She then suggested that I might call the people who manufactured the typesetting equipment and that perhaps they might be helpful. She also suggested that perhaps they could make us the italic font and in my anger and frustration at this new interruption, I asked, 'who thought up these new instructions'? As usual, she replied, 'Jesus and The Holy Spirit, of course'. I remember replying, . . . so now they're typesetters as well.

That afternoon I found myself calling the manufacturer of the typesetting equipment, located in Massachusetts and asking for the director of public relations. After explaining my problem to this gentleman, that when I had originally ordered this particular type font, that they had not yet at that time struck the italic and that I could not proceed with the printing, until certain passages, were changed to italic and that I was facing a serious delay of finishing the books. He listened patiently to my tale of woe, and then said, 'boy, are you lucky'. I responded, 'why am I lucky'? He replied, 'we just struck that particular type font, last week, and if you order it today, it will be airmailed to you immediately, so that you will have it tomorrow . . . and . . . furthermore, you will receive a full fifty percent discount, on the font'. Wow I thought, what timing. I wondered about this whole episode, quickly ordered the italic and started to believe, for the very first time, since this whole thing had started, that this Course In Miracles, might really have some 'special stuff', connected to it. I also figured that since this material was supposed to have been given to Helen by none other than a guy named Jesus . . . and . . . that Jesus was supposed to have been Jewish, it figured, that he loved a bargain as much as I did and that he had actually waited, till the type was made, before asking us to buy it, so that we could get our italic . . . with a discount.

The typesetting was now complete and another miracle occurred. I found a binder in nearby New Jersey who actually did smythe sewing. I arranged to see him at his plant, a place called Quinn and Bowden. My appointment was with the president, a young man by the name of Michael Quinn and soon after I arrived, I was ushered into his office and he greeted me with a cheerful, Hi Laddie. We spoke for a short time and I outlined what I was wanting, in the way of gold leaf stamping, cover material etc. and he assured me that there was no problems, that he could foresee. I then turned over the mechanicals on the three books and he called in his head estimator to determine what the costs would be. While waiting for the figures to come back from estimating, Michael Quinn and I started talking about the materials. I told him that I didn't understand a word of what was contained in the three books, but the people, 'the family', truly believed in its authenticity and that it would really help a lot of people.

Mike's estimator came back with the figures, Michael looked at them and said, 'these numbers look good', I looked at them, agreed to the numbers and we shook hands. Michael then asked me when I would need delivery of the books and I thought about the conversation I had had with Judy the night before and I had asked her when she needed to have books in her hands and she had informed me that the week of the twentieth of June, would be perfect as she was going out to California and would love to get the books into the hands of many of the people who had been patiently awaiting their arrival. Since it was already April of 1976, I told her immediately that there was very little possibility of completion of these books by June of the same year, but Judy had urged in a most loving manner and I answered Mike Quinn with 'the twentieth of June would be fine'. Mike looked at me and said, 'no problem, Saul' and asked me to follow him into his scheduling room. When we entered the scheduling room, it looked like a library, complete with rolling ladders, along the walls and instead of book shelves, each of the walls had a floor to ceiling blackboard, filled with schedules and production dates. Mike climbed up on a ladder and started to write on the top of the blackboard:

A COURSE IN MIRACLES . . . . Book I Text
A COURSE IN MIRACLES . . . . Book II Workbook
A COURSE IN MIRACLES . . . . Book III Teachers Manual

I shouted to Mike Quinn, hold up a moment, he turned around, looking down at me from the top of the ladder and he asked, 'what's wrong Laddie'? I replied, . . . 'Mike you're in the wrong year'. He was entering the delivery date into the month of June, 1977, instead of June of 1976. Mike jumped off of the top step of the ladder and doubled up with laughter. I asked him why he was laughing and he said, 'come with me Laddie'. He led me to the other side of the room and he asked me to read the names of the publishing companies all scheduled in 1976. The list of names read like a who's who in the field of publishing and he then asked me if I was asking him to put my three books in front of some of the best known publishing houses in the world. Remembering Judy's request the night before, I replied, 'well it would be nice'. He looked at me, now quite serious and he said, 'the books stay in the delivery slot of June, 1977 or you had better take them somewhere else. 'Wait a minute, I said, your company is the best and since everything was agreeable up to now, could you at least try for a better delivery date'? I added, 'I didn't say it had to be done by the twentieth of June of this year, I only said, it would be nice, so maybe you can do a little better. Mike replied in a somewhat angry voice and said, if you want us to do these books, the delivery is most definitely, the end of June, 1977. 1 looked at him and figured it's worth one more try and I said, 'let me call you tomorrow morning, perhaps you'll be able to make a change here and there in your schedule, for us'. Stubbornly, he said, 'the delivery date stands, June of 1977'. We shook hands and I left to go back to my office on Long Island. I felt badly that I would have to tell Judy and 'the family' that they would have to wait for books for more than another year but I felt, I had done my best. That night, I felt really uncomfortable about calling Judy and I decided that I'd take one more crack at Michael Quinn, the next morning before making my call to Judy.

At nine forty five the next morning, I called Mike Quinn and inquired as to whether he perhaps had found a way of giving me a better delivery. He replied, 'you son of a gun'. I inquired, why was I a son of a gun and he responded and said, that yesterday, after I had left, he did something, that he had never done before. He said that he knew that his wife was into this kind of 'stuff' and that he had taken my mechanical proofs, home with him, to show to her. At their dinner table, he continued, as she was going through the material, she had asked Mike, 'who were the Authors' and how did the material come about Mike told her the little bit he knew and she kept leafing through page after page. Mike then shared with his wife the confusion of our delivery dates and she asked Mike to try and help to get these materials, out as soon as possible. Mike then related to me, that she repeated to him, that he must try to help get these books out into the world as quickly as possible, that it was truly important. Again as he described it to me, he refused and she then started with the heavy duty ammunition, a more powerful persuader. She asked Mike if they didn't enjoy a happy, lovely married life. Mike responded, 'well yes we do'. She then went on to say, 'well it won't be nearly as lovely, if you don't help these people'.

Our three books were indeed completed on the twenty first of June, in 1976 and there was a party held at the home of Judy and Bob Skutch, on the evening of the twenty second of June, 1976. Everyone involved was there that evening and I got to meet numbers one through six and number ten, as well. Present at the party was a lovely Maryknoll Nun by the name of Sister Charlotte and Judy Skutch had asked her to prepare beautiful framed paintings in numerous colors, for everyone involved with the production of the book. Mine stated . . .

With Gratitude

The time you spent is given back to you
In shining hours and in quiet peace.
The care you gave to God He saves for you
With loving kindness so your sorrows cease.

Your patience is His Own, and comes to you
When you have need of it. But only look
Upon His smile, and you will understand
How very much, He thanks you for His book.

The next morning, I put Judy Skutch on a plane bound for San Francisco, California with three hundred completed sets of A Course In Miracles.

Since I did not have a warehouse to store the materials, my greatest concern became, what was to become of the five thousand sets of books I had printed. I felt that I needed to come up with a plan, to help sell those unknown books and I conceived a brilliant plan. Being an advertising person, I would put together an ad, which I perceived would run in the Sunday New York Times Book Review, which would surely sell all of the books immediately. I could hardly wait for the three weeks that Judy was away, so that I could share this marvelous plan with her. The day after she got back from California, I called her and told her what I had put together and how we could sell everyone of the five thousand sets of A Course In Miracles, immediately. She listened patiently as I outlined how the ad stated that the world now had a set of three 'how to' books from none other than Jesus and The Holy Spirit on how to eliminate guilt and fear, from everyone's life. Judy listened and as soon as I had finished sharing my fabulous plan on the way to sell five thousand sets of books, Judy lovingly responded, 'no Saul, that's not the way . . it will happen'. She went on to say, 'that those people who are ready to receive this material, would know it, without any form of advertising, and that they are already, being informed by Jesus and The Holy Spirit and that no game plan for sales, was needed'. Clearly, this woman was demented. She was actually telling me that she and the family' believed that forty seven hundred sets of books, would sell themselves, without benefit of advertising. I put down the phone, very much disillusioned and I sincerely believed that I would be stuck with forty seven hundred sets of A Course In Miracles, for the rest of my days, without a warehouse.

Well once again, Judy, was right. Within the first year, with nothing but word of mouth all five thousand sets of A Course In Miracles were gone and Bob Skutch ordered the second printing which was for seventy five hundred sets, with one major change. Dr. Helen saw that the light blue denim covers were indeed marking and not holding up well and asked me to go to the darker blue lexitone, that I had originally suggested and the Course is still being bound with the same material.

By the way, Jesus and The Holy Spirit helped to get us a much needed warehouse in 1980, when the print orders, from Bob Skutch were up to twenty thousand sets of A Course In Miracles at a time and the rest as they say . . . is history.

My Thoughts

Psychotherapy and A Course In Miracles

About six months after I completed the printing of A Course In Miracles, I was asked by Judy and Bob to print a fourth book entitled Psychotherapy, Purpose, Process and Practice.

Helen and Bill felt, that since the Course, was a Course in Spiritual Healing, there was a definite need for a book, outlining the role of the therapist. Since all of us, without exception, are in the truest sense, GOD'S therapists, the book Psychotherapy, Purpose, Process and Practice, was written and printed for all of us. This book was also given to Helen, and Bill by the very same Source, as the Course, that Source being Jesus and the Holy Spirit.

The book opens with:

'Psychotherapy is the only form of therapy there is. Since only the mind can be sick, only the mind can be healed. Only the mind is in need of healing. This does not appear to be the case, for the manifestations of this world seem real indeed. Psychotherapy is necessary so that an individual can begin to question their reality. Sometimes he is able to start to open his mind without formal help, but even then it is always some change in his interpersonal relationships that enables him to do so. Sometimes he needs a more structured extended relationship with an 'official' therapist. Either way, the task is the same; the patient must be helped to change his mind about the 'reality' of illusions.'

The above paragraph, which opens the Psychotherapy book, are perhaps the most important words ever given to us and it is my belief that it is the answer to all illness, problems and relationships. Probably since time began, we have been trying to understand, why we get sick, why things sometimes don't go right and why we sometimes don't get along with those we love. The answer if the above is correct and I believe it is, is most definitely the mind. It has now been clarified for us by none other than Jesus and the Holy Spirit, that there are no accidents, that everything that seems to happen to us, happens not by accident but is happening because their is a learning opportunity in every event, every relationship and even every problem.

---

*Psycotherapy, Purpose, Process and Practice is published by The Foundation For Inner Peace, Glen Ellen, CA.

The word 'official' in the above paragraph should also be addressed. It is suggesting that it is no accident that some person or event enters into your life, in order to help you to learn the particular lesson, you may have come into this incarnation to learn.

The Course also makes it quite clear that each and everyone of us is a Psychotherapist and that we all are in 'training' to perhaps get it right. While we are on the subject of 'we', for those of us that are brand new to the Course, it is absolutely essential to understand that the Course, while it seems to be written in a male oriented language, the Course or Psychotherapy Book are not meant to infer gender of any description. The Course is not at all about male or female, his or her, boy or girl or even man or woman, it is absolutely inferring that we all, without exception are . . .

beautiful children of a Loving Father/Mother/GOD …
in whom, She/He, are well pleased.

Make no mistake about it, the Course is definitely not sexist and it can only retard your progress in understanding the message that the Course delivers, if you think it is.

Notice in the second sentence of the opening paragraph of the Psychotherapy booklet, that it states:

'Since only the mind can be sick, only the mind can be healed'
Followed by:

'Only the mind is in need of healing.'

This can be shown with a simple exercise, I use in my lectures. Let's try this simple exercise together: Please close your eyes and visualize or picture, if you can, your brain. Get a clear picture and after you get that picture, open your eyes. Most of us, I have found, have little or no problem, picturing our brain.

I then ask everyone and will now ask you the reader, to close your eyes once again and this time, picture your mind. Generally, most everyone in my audiences smile and the result, every single time, is that few if any of the folks sitting in front of me, are able to get a picture, any kind of picture, of their mind. Try it.

While the image of the brain comes instantly to most of us, the image of the mind, doesn't seem to come at all. Does that mean, that we don't have a mind? Certainly not. The Course and the Psychotherapy booklet make it very clear, that, not only do we have a mind, surprisingly to most of us, we are told we have two minds. Actually it is really only one mind but we are informed that this one mind is actually a 'split' mind, each having its' own function. The minds are identified in the Course as the GOD Mind and the other mind is identified in the Course, as the ego mind.

Notice that when talking about the GOD Mind a capital M is used and when reference is made to the ego mind, a lower case m is used. When I was setting the type for A Course In Miracles, way back in 1975, this business of where to capitalize and where not to capitalize gave me the most problems. I simply did not understand that everything which refers to GOD, in the Course, is always capitalized and everything which refers to ego, is not capitalized.

What the Course is trying to show us is, that the GOD mind is always trying to lead us in the right direction, or correct path, while the ego part of mind is always trying to lead us in the opposite direction. The Course uses the word Mind and it also uses the word Holy Spirit. Both are actually the same and if a third clarifying word is needed, you can substitute the word Soul, if you find it helpful. Now for the good part. The GOD Mind we are told, is on the job with us, twenty four hours of every day and is available to us, to help us, to guide us and to be there for us, whenever we ask for the help. There is one thing that you need to know and that is that the help, the guidance, the wisdom, the direction will not come, according to the Course, unless it is asked for, requested or prayed for. The Holy Spirit, or, capital M Mind, will not come to help, unless it is invited. Make no mistake about it though, H.S. as I now call Mind, is most definitely on the job, twenty four hours a day, seven days a week, all of your life. Contrary to a lot of folks that I meet who are studying the Course, many people say to me that 'well I don't want to bother the Holy Spirit with trivial unimportant things' and my understanding of the Course is, that there is no such thought, or idea, or action that is too trivial and the Course clearly states that with the Holy Spirit's help, we can do anything, and that on our own, without that help, we can do nothing.

Now in the case of the ego mind, we are told that it is in direct conflict with anything that the GOD Mind is telling us and while it is also on the job, twenty four hours a day, the ego mind is forever trying to prove to us that 'we are not, beautiful children of GOD', but that we are our bodies, that we appear to be. So that everything that appears to go on with and through our bodies, our ego mind would have us believe, that there is no way, that we are, or can be . . . what or whom, we truly are . . . that perfect Child of GOD.

So we have this 'split belief', that we are sometimes, beautifully in 'sync' with GOD and at other times, we are not. If this is still confusing to you, let's do another simple exercise which might make it a bit easier to understand.

Visualize your two arms extended straight out, from your body. Imagine that at the end of your left arm is the GOD Mind and at the end of your right arm is the ego mind. Let us now think, that since we got into our bodies, we have spent half of our time listening to the dictates of the GOD Mind and the other fifty percent of our lives, listening to the ego mind. The choice of which mind we chose to listen to, was and always is, up to ourselves. Now continuing with this exercise, let us assume, that the fifty percent of our time, spent in listening to the GOD Mind has resulted in all of the happy, healthy, abundant and good things that have occurred in our lives. On the other hand, when we have followed the path of the ego the other fifty percent of the time, those reflect the times that we spent in confusion, illness, anger, pain, suffering and just about any other negative emotion or action, one could have. Now, getting back to your two outstretched arms, what I want you to understand is that as you start to question which thought system you seem to be listening to, without your even realizing it, there starts to occur a shift in your thinking. In other words, just by becoming aware that you can control what's going on in your life, the shift very gradually starts to, in some way, change things that seem to be happening. The shift is actually taking you from a place of wrong minded thinking to right minded thinking, or, to put it in Course language, we start hearing the voice for GOD, the Holy Spirit, more than we are hearing the voice of ego. Ultimately what occurs is that the shift in perception that I'm talking about results in now those two outstretched arms (representing Holy Spirit and ego) now start to move and we now see the left arm a little higher and the right arm a little lower. Putting that into an imaginary fraction, let us say that we are now hearing the voice for GOD fifty two percent of the time, and the voice for ego forty eight percent of the time. As we become more and more aware of this happening, imagine if you will, that there is a gradual shifting and to use the fractions once again, we could find ourselves listening and hearing the voice of GOD (H.S.) fifty five percent of the time and the voice for ego, forty five percent of the time.

So the question becomes, do we ever make the complete shift, in other words, do we ever only hear the voice for GOD, one hundred percent of the time and not hear from the ego at all. I must tell you that I have been with this Course now since 1975 and I have yet to meet a single person who has completely, one hundred percent, been able to make the complete shift, so that they no longer hear the voice of ego, at all. The only one according to my understanding of the Course, who has accomplished this and has given us this wisdom, and has completely transcended the ego, is our elder brother, Jesus. To those of us of the Jewish faith, there may be and probably is, a great deal of discomfort, whenever the name Jesus is spoken. I have met thousands of people of the Jewish faith at my talks and lectures that cringe everytime I mention the name of Jesus and it really doesn't surprise me at all, since I was one of those people. Being of the Jewish faith myself, I can tell you most assuredly that in the Bronx of New York, where I grew up, Jesus was not one of the most popular guys, on our block. He certainly was not the man who I would think of as a role model, for me or anyone of my other friends, who were also Jewish, with the exception of my cousin Paul.

Getting back to the Psychotherapy and A Course In Miracles, both say that 'the purpose of Psychotherapy is to remove the blocks to truth and it's aim is to aid the patient (all of us) in abandoning our fixed delusional system. We are then told, that every single one of us, without exception, regardless of our form of distress, are attacking ourselves and our peace of mind, is suffering as a result and once we learn to call upon the Holy Spirit for help, the guarantee is, that it will come.' Psychotherapy, then is a process of changing which part of mind, we will choose to listen to. The belief that all healing is of GOD, through the GOD Mind starts to occur when each of us starts to see the perfection in each of us and when we can truly bless each other, we again are guaranteed, that we then open ourselves to receive the peace of GOD. Surprisingly, the Psycho-therapy informs us that we don't even have to be religious or believe in GOD, but it does state that we must teach and practice forgiveness rather than condemnation. The only true therapist, it's pointed out,

*Psycotherapy, Purpose, Process and Practice is published by The Foundation For Inner Peace, Glen Ellen, CA.

-31-

would be a therapist that does not possess an ego and as pointed out before, I don't know of too many (none except Jesus) who answer that description.

The Psychotherapy Book points out that all illness is mental illness and that sickness is insanity, because all sickness is mental illness and in order to have healing, one must ask for the Holy Spirit's help, without time limits, without unforgiveness and certainly without fear, that it might not happen. Psychotherapy is without a doubt forgiveness. Forgiveness is the bottom line of the Course and without forgiveness, it is very clear, there can be no healing and remember, that sickness is just another form of unforgiveness. Fear and guilt which are really one and the same are the reasons and once we learn to turn them over to the Holy Spirit, they can at last be gone. As for all of us being therapists, which we are told we are, it is important to understand that we don't have to do anything, or take any type of action, that indeed, everything will be arranged for us, by the Holy Spirit and that the moment we stop making judgements of any type, the healing, can and does occur. The Psychotherapy Book then goes on to explain that no one, can buy or pay for healing, because all Healing Is Through GOD and only GOD and further . . . is guaranteed by GOD.

So remember, the Holy Spirit is always, without fail, there for you and as the Course and the Psychotherapy Book reminds us, GOD'S only wish for every single one of us, without exception, is, to restore us to a place of peace, joy and happiness.

*Psycotherapy, Purpose, Process and Practice is published by The Foundation For Inner Peace, Glen Ellen, CA.
*A Course In Miracles is published by the Foundation For Inner Peace, Glen Ellen, CA.

What's Of GOD . . . What's Of ego

If you still are finding some confusion as to the split mind, perhaps I can make it a little more understandable by clarifying GOD and the ego in a little more detail. The Course tells us specifically that if it isn't GOD, then it must be the ego. Those two are the only two parts of our minds that really control what we are all about. Simply put, if we listen to our GOD Mind, we stay out of trouble and our lives seem to work. If we listen to the ego mind, everything goes wrong and our lives don't work. In short the ego is a part of mind, which we ourselves made and it is not real. It is constantly trying to create the illusion that we, every single one of us, without exception, is separated from GOD. Nothing, according to the Course, could be further from the truth. The Course explains to us that this whole experience, that we seem to be living through, is nothing but a great big dream, or as the Course puts it, an illusion, with GOD being the only reality and ego, just a part of the dream. Another way of looking at this difficult to believe concept is, that the truth is, that we are all children of GOD, fast asleep in GOD's house and that all of the events occurring are not really happening to us at all. It's just a dream. Now let me tell you that for me to accept what I've just written, took me the better part of two years to accept and it was not a comfortable idea for me to accept, even after I started to believe, what I've just conveyed. In order to make it easier to understand when I do my lectures entitled All Healing Is Through GOD, I use another exercise that I have made up, which seems to be helpful and it goes like this:

Let's assume that we all (for the sake of this exercise) have a favorite Uncle Louis. This Uncle Louis is the greatest, most wonderful uncle, we can imagine. He's the uncle that always seems to be there when we need help, he's the uncle that lends us the money when we can't pay the rent, he's the uncle that bails us out of any trouble, we seem to get ourselves into. Now for the sake of clarifying this whole exercise, we need to imagine that each and everyone of us, had the very same dream last night and it was a nightmare. There doesn't seem to be anyone at my lectures, who hasn't experienced a nightmare once in awhile, so I'll presume that anyone reading this book, has also had an occasional nightmare. Now in our nightmare, last night, our favorite Uncle Louis was chasing us with a huge caveman type of club and as if that weren't bad enough, the club had long razor sharp, pointy spikes, coming out the end of the thick part of the club and here in our nightmare is our favorite Uncle Louis, chasing us at top speed, seemingly wanting to swat us with all of his might and . . . he's gaining on us. Just as he's about to catch up with us and swing that club into our backside, with all of his strength, we give out with a mighty scream, loud enough to even wake ourselves up and through that dream, that nightmare, that horrible frightening experience, we may have hyperventilated, broke out in a cold sweat or just have been scared out of our wits. We suddenly sit up in our beds, wipe our brow and say, whew, am I glad that was just a dream, that it wasn't real, that it was all an illusion. We then get up and go about our business and probably never even mention the nightmare to our Uncle Louis.

What the Course is trying to tell us, is that this whole experience, is just like the Uncle Louis experience, in short it's not real. Now we also learn, that we can and do have happy dreams and what this whole learning, teaching experience is trying to convey, is that the choice is most definitely up to us. Who would opt to have ego Uncle Louis type nightmares, rather than happy dreams, which are always supplied by the Holy Spirit, without fail.

Now what came as a surprise to me, is that GOD never even recognizes the illusion, the big dream, because the reality is, that no separation, between ourselves and GOD, actually ever occurred. It too is all part of the ego's thinking and the ego is forever trying to have us believe, that we actually could and did, separate from our Father/Mother, GOD. It never really happened. At the beginning of the Course in Book I, the Text, it states that Adam, went into a deep sleep, but nowhere does it say that he's woken up as yet. The idea that GOD is a vengeful, punishing GOD has been given to us, when what the truth is, is clearly stated in the Course, that GOD never condemns, therefore, GOD never punishes. Never. How many people that you know, when confronted with seeming tragedy, look up to the heavens and cry, oh GOD, what did I do, what did she do, what did he do, to deserve such cruel and inhuman punishment.

Heaven and hell do not really exist. They are a state of mind that we have created. The proof of that is certainly that two people

---

*Book I, Text of A Course In Miracles is published by The Foundation For Inner Peace, Glen Ellen, CA.

can have the very same things going on in their lives (dreams), one person handles whatever comes up, the other person commits suicide, believing that he/she is a worthless sinner, that GOD will ultimately punish for the bad things, he or she has done. Once again, it's called guilt or it's called fear, it doesn't really matter as both are exactly the same thing . . . ego.

Our only real true identity is the one mentioned before and if I seem to keep repeating it over and over again it is simply because it is something that we need to remember. That identity is that . . . *We are beautiful children of a Loving Mother/Father/GOD, in whom, She/He, is well pleased..* Our reality is . . . that we are perfect, as is GOD.

My Thoughts

The Ego Conspiracy

In July of 1986, I printed a book for a man by the name of Chuck Okerstrom. Chuck is a retired NASA space engineer, living with his wife Glenda in Titusville, Florida and in between lecturing, teaching classes on A Course In Miracles and his annual three month trips all over this country and Canada, Chuck has become very well known as a teacher of the Course and I have heard some people say, that Chuck's audio tapes on the Course, are as clear as any tapes that have ever been done. To my mind, The Ego Conspiracy explains the ego as well or better than any other book I have read and at my lectures I read the following excerpt, from Chapter Four.

'We have now learned there are two ways of thinking, and which way we choose determines what experiences we will have in our lives. What may not be clear to us yet, is the fact that it will also establish the kind of world we perceive, as existing here and now. We have learned there is a perfect law of cause and effect. What we may not yet understand is that this universal law is so powerful and so all-encompassing that it literally transforms the world we perceive each second of our lives, so that the events taking place and the effects we experience will always be exactly like the thoughts we have and believe to be true. At this point, some readers may be saying, Oh, come on! We can t go along with that. That's really going off the deep end if the whole world is going to change just to match our thoughts. How can this be happening when there are billions of people, each having thoughts that most likely are different from ours. Calm down a minute, and try to understand two very important words that were overlooked. First, were talking about the world that each of us PERCEIVES, not what might or might not exist. Second, and this one is very, very important, it's only those thoughts that we really and truly BELIEVE to be true that count. From A Course In Miracles, we are given another law by which we live in this world of perception. It is called perception's fundamental law and it states, 'you see what you believe is there and you believe it is there because you want it there'. Again, some readers may reply, 'That still doesn't make sense! If we

* The Ego Conspiracy, Chuck Okerstrom, Mind and Miracles, Ft. Lauderdale, FL.
* A Course in Miracles, Foundation For Inner Peace, Glen Ellen, CA.

look out and see evil occurring, the law says it's because we want this wrong to be happening! We can t buy that. We didn't have anything to do with the evil being committed by others.'

We have to approach this law with an open mind if we are going to clearly understand its meaning. We need to remember, first of all, that it is our choice which thought system we believe is true and accept as the way we're going to interpret the information coming from our five senses. If we choose to use the ego thought system, we're operating from a basis of sin and guilt. In that case, we believe that everyone is guilty of sinning and needs to be punished. As we discussed earlier in Chapter Two, we don't like this guilty feeling and desire desperately to get rid of it. The easiest way to do this is to try to find others that appear to be more sinful than we are, thus making us feel we are better than they.

From this point of view, let's rewrite the law for this specific case. It now would read, 'we see sin (wrong) being done by others because we believe we are all guilty of sinning, and we believe that if it is taking place out there and we're not a part of it, then this will make us feel good about ourselves.
I know many readers feel they have no such intentions in their minds when they see wrong occurring. I'm sure, on the surface, all of us feel the same way. This is all part of the cover-up plan in the ego thought system. If we consciously knew this was the reason we were judging and condemning others, then our feelings of guilt would not be temporarily taken away. Our ego thought system does its job very nicely by convincing us in our conscious minds that all we really want is to have 'Justice' done and to rid our world of all wrong doing.'

The above is quoted from Chuck's book and it is, I think, a clear and concise couple of paragraphs that explain beautifully in my opinion, how and perhaps what makes the ego rather tricky. Before anyone gets confused, let me state that the Course ego as discussed is different from the ego that we have been taught about, since childhood. The Course ego is our negative thought system, totally opposed to the truth, that we are all, indeed beautiful children of a

Loving GOD, Who is perfectly pleased with each and every one of us. The Freudian ego, that we all have grown up with, is the ego that seems to push us to putting on a clean shirt, or suit or skirt, brushing our hair, and reminding us that we should look our best to feel our best. Both ego's are illusions, both are false, both are not responsible for how we feel, or, who we truly are.

My Thoughts

Jesus and Death

One of the most important lessons I have learned from the Course, is that there is no death. What the Course would have us believe, is, that we do not die and that the man who gave us, and the world the very best demonstration was our elder brother Jesus. In the Course, it is made very clear, that Jesus, did not die for our sins, as many other philosophies would have us believe, but rather that number one, he did not die at all and number two, how better could he demonstrate, the truth that there is no death. In the Course we are told that Jesus is the name of a man who was able to see the face of Christ, in everyone of his brothers and sisters and indeed it makes the point, that not only is Jesus a Christ (of the Light) but that we all (without exception) are also Christs, as well. In my lectures I point out to make this point, that it would be and as well pefectly ok, to think of ourselves as Christs, because that is our true identity.

I've given this whole concept a great deal of thought, since my introduction to the Course in 1975 and of course, coming from the Jewish faith, my first thoughts while setting the type on A Course In Miracles, was, what a crock. As a matter of fact up until the Course, I had absolutely no belief that a man named Jesus really even existed, but as a kid growing up in the Bronx of New York City, if I did think about Jesus or hear the name, I somehow, in someway, held him personally responsible, for all of the trials, tribulations, murders, anti-semitism, of the Jewish people as a whole, down through the ages. How wrong I was. What I know now, is that this man was trying to teach three things and three things only. Those three things are, without a doubt . . . LOVE, FORGIVENESS and That There Is No Death.

When the very first group of A Course In Miracles was started in my office way back in 1977, I can remember squirming in my seat as my cousin Paul would have each of the fourteen people present, take a turn, at reading a paragraph at a time, from the three books. Invariably, every time the name Jesus or the Holy Spirit was read or mentioned, it was like someone running chalk on a blackboard, for me. It took about seven weeks, for Paul to pick up my discomfort and my annoyance to Jesus and the Holy Spirit and finally he grabbed me

A Course in Miracles is published by the Foundation For Inner Peace, Glen Ellen, CA.

-41-

one evening after a meeting and said, 'Spank, you're still really quite uncomfortable with Jesus, aren't you?' I replied, 'yes, I really am'. Paul, seeming to understand my biased thinking, said, 'I think I can help you.' He said, 'whenever you hear the name Jesus, just transfer that thought, that name and call him by his real name'. I looked at Paul, my cousin the lunatic and puzzled and confused, said to him, 'what the hell are you talking about?' Paul, always, well most of the time, calm, cool, collected and smiling, said, 'Jesus, is not his real name, at least, not when he was born'. Again, without breaking my stare, feeling just a bit uncomfortable, just talking about Jesus, again I asked, 'are you telling me that Jesus was not named Jesus at birth'? 'That's right,' Paul answered, 'Jesus was not named Jesus at birth'. Totally confused and puzzled, I asked, 'what was his name at birth', knowing that a joke was sure to come from Paul's lips. Still smiling, Paul quietly answered, 'Jesus's name at birth was Immanuel.' 'So,' he continued, 'perhaps it would be easier for you, whenever the name Jesus, is used, just substitute his real name, Immanuel.' 'You're putting me on Paul, aren't you, one of your crappy jokes, right? 'Nope,' Paul answered, 'that's the truth, it's for real'. Not really convinced, I figured that if Paul wasn't laughing, maybe he wasn't pulling my leg and since all this Jesus stuff was bugging me, as it was, let me give it a try. So, for the next three or four weeks, I substituted the name Immanuel, every time I heard the name Jesus mentioned.

It didn't help, I still found myself getting annoyed at the mere mention of the name Jesus and even with my trying to quickly change the name in my head, from Jesus to Immanuel, it seemed more annoying with each passing day. Paul picked up on my confusion and again, after one of our meetings said, 'you're still having a rough time with Jesus and Immanuel, aren't you?' 'You better believe it, I can't let go of all of the anger I must be carrying around, over this guy Jesus, I mean Immanuel.' Paul, again smiling, very relaxed, said, 'well there is another thing you can do to get rid of this anger and fear'. 'What's that', I asked? 'Well, just think of him and this time change his name Jesus and Immanuel and use his nickname'. 'His nickname' and this time I was sure he was putting me on, one of his crazy jokes, more nonsense 'what kind of nickname?' I asked. With the straightest of faces, Paul looked straight at me, eyes to eyes and answered, 'just call him Manny, he won't mind'. I grew up in the Bronx with friends named Manny. So for the next two years, for me, Jesus was Manny. Paul's suggestion worked and all of my prejudice, was gone as though it never had existed.

As my study of the Course continued, I learned that Jesus was on this earthly plane for a specific purpose. That purpose has been misconstrued for many years as far as I can determine, since it appears to me, that most of the people I used to meet before my involvement with the Course, were believing that Jesus's mission was the crucifixion. What the Course has taught me, is that the mission of Jesus was plainly not the crucifixion, but plainly, it was the Resurrection, which plainly teaches, the world and everyone in it, that there is no death.

It also became quite clear to me, even as a beginning student that while the world believes that while the crucifixion was going on and we're told that Jesus put up no defense and his best friends begged him to defend himself, I now believe that Jesus knew precisely what he was doing every step of the way and he had logiced out, that by appearing to die on the cross, and then appearing and actually being alive, this would prove beyond a shadow of a doubt, that there is no death. Can anyone truly believe, that a teacher of GOD, on the level of Jesus, could not jump off of a cross, at any time, he wished. Consider the nature of the other lessons he taught, and is credited with. It had to be, that his desire or plan, plainly was to show, to prove, that there is no death, that contrary to our beliefs, we don't die.

Additionally, what better way could he show that any act committed by any brother, is forgivable. Jesus's message, clearly and simply is . . . Love and Forgiveness and that We Do Not Die. When we leave this form, we still are living . . . and it is only the body, that dies. Since we are not our bodies but are Spirit, we go on.

The Course teaches us that everything of GOD, is permanent, forever. That means us, you and me, without exception. What happens when the mind tells the body, that it is time to leave the body (whenever we choose that time), what goes in the ground, in the box, or the cremation is not, I repeat not, you or I, it is our body . . . not our mind. If you can accept this and I didn't for several years, you will have no difficulty in accepting that it is the mind that goes on to

* A Course in Miracles is published by the Foundation For Inner Peace, Glen Ellen, CA.

the next experience, while the brain, just like the rest of our bodies, eventually turns to dust.

The Course does not talk about the next experience, or the next after that. You see, the Course deals only in the now, simply because the lessons provided in the Course are wanting you, are alerting you, to make now, the only time there is. Jesus and the Holy Spirit are wanting this big dream, to be the happiest big dream, you and I can have. That's right this whole illusion as the Course puts it, can be the happiest illusion, a happy dream or a nightmare, it is all up to us. The sickness, the unhappiness and even the death, is all an illusion, a great big fat dream.

Remember . . . the NOW.

---

*A Course in Miracles is published by the Foundation For Inner Peace, Glen Ellen, CA.

The Mind and the mind

Throughout the Course we see the word mind appear with a capital M and it also appear with a small m. As I've indicated in the beginning of this book, all through the Course, everything that is capitalized is of GOD, and when we see the same word not capitalized, that is telling us, that it is not of GOD. To put it another way, when we listen to the Holy Spirit, we are listening to, or following the guidance of Mind and when we listen to our ego, we are listening to mind. Mind will always, without exception, guide us down the correct direction, will help us make the right decision, and always, also without exception, refers to GOD, Christ, Spirit and the true us. On the other hand, mind, always follows the dictates of the ego and any time we find ourselves in any type of difficulty such as illness, guilt, anger or even death, make no mistake about it, we are listening to our ego mind. The Course tells us that Mind being of GOD, is real and mind being of ego, is illusion. Depending on which mind we listen to, we can make the right decision or . . . the wrong decision.

One of the things I believe to be absolutely true, is, that either mind, or Mind completely control the body, and that at no time, does the body, ever, control our mind, or our Mind. For me, listening more and more to the Guidance of the GOD Mind, has actually allowed me to stay in perfect health, never having or wanting to seek a doctor's aid or assistance. It has also given me the ability to give up my Blue Cross, ten years ago and to not spend a cent on aspirin, drugs or as the Course puts it, not to depend on magic, for my feeling wonderful, year after year after year. I have come to believe that what goes on in mind, somehow finds expression, in the body and that in order for our ego to prove to us that we are our bodies, (which we are not), is forever trying to prove to us, that we are *not* perfect children of GOD (which we most definitely are). As we approach a certain age, most of us find ourselves being thoroughly brain washed that age or years spent in our particular body, has the ability to determine that certain things must go wrong with our bodies. For instance, when we reach forty, it is supposed to be all downhill, according to most of the hype put out by Madison Avenue. People who never had a need of glasses before, suddenly change their mind

* A Course in Miracles is published by the Foundation For Inner Peace, Glen Ellen, CA.

and find themselves believing that they now cannot exist another day, without glasses. Billions of dollars are spent each year on cosmetics, diet remedies, drugs and other paraphernalia, by people everywhere, who believe that the answers to their supposed problems, will magically disappear with the magic. It doesn't work, save your money and just try listening to your Mind, instead of your mind.

Orthodox medicine will tell you that 'it is to be expected,' but is it really? When one 'expects' to have to wear eyeglasses at a certain age, is that truly your eyes giving your mind the message, as we have been taught it is, or is it not, really your mind giving your eyes the message that your time has come and that you won't, can't function at all, without the glasses. It is your ego mind telling you, reminding you, that your body cannot function without the magic glasses. When I stopped wearing the eyeglasses, that I had worn for many years, what really happened? Since you've asked, I'll tell you. I started my printing career at the age of twelve and one half and spent many years learning how to set type and also did a tremendous amount of proof reading. Everyone that worked in the printing plant that I worked at, without exception, wore eyeglasses. It was expected, believed by all I'm sure, to be necessary and I guess the belief was that one could do a good job, only if one could see the print clearly and the only way one could see the print clearly, was through the aid of eyeglasses. I had never needed glasses before and in school, everytime my eyes were tested, they tested twenty,twenty. I can remember there was a sense of pride, after reading the required line, to receive the grade of twenty, twenty and I went along knowing that my eyes were perfect. Soon after my starting in the printing plant, I changed my mind, my ego mind told me that my eyes were no longer perfect. With all the typesetting and proofreading I was doing, how could I not be straining my eyes and all of a sudden, even at the age of twelve and a half, my ego mind had me convinced that I couldn't function without the aid and assistance of eyeglasses. I put on glasses and didn't take them off until 1983, when I finally started to listen to the voice for GOD, the Holy Spirit, the GOD Mind.

When I stopped wearing the glasses that I had worn for so many years, what really happened was that I stopped listening to my ego mind and started listening to my true Mind. The day I decided to remove my glasses, I was determined to do so because I recognized that I had made the glasses a crutch, which I had created a dependency for. In all the years up until 1983, the only time the glasses came off of my face, was when I got into bed to go to sleep. How could I just take them off never to have need of them again, you ask, well the answer is as simple as I'm making it sound. The only way it can be done, that I know of, is to start listening to the Mind, instead of the mind.

This example that I have given to you in this chapter not only deals with eyeglasses, I use the very same principals, to improve my quality of life, even in this illusion, for everything that I feel I need to do. However, I must make it clear that although the Course is a course in showing you how to recognize and give up the magic (should you choose to) in no way does the Course recommend that you must, give up the magic. There are no musts in the Course, that I know of and what is explained by Jesus and the Holy Spirit is, that if you feel there is any, I repeat any need for the magic, the doctor, the aspirin, the chemotherapy, the valium, the vitamins, the special diets, the glasses . . . stay with whatever you are doing, or taking, because at this point, you still have need of the magic. Do not let my experience, dictate, what your experience, should or could be. Judy Skutch pointed out to me, way back in 1976, that there are many, many roads to GOD and that A Course In Miracles, was only one road to GOD. If all of this doesn't feel or seem to work for you, find another road to GOD for yourself, that will work for you. While it is true, that this Course In Miracles has captivated the thinking and actions of many people like you and me, it is also true, that many find they just can't buy into any of these concepts. What I do is Love them and bless them and ASK the Holy Spirit to let them find their way, through Mind.

My Thoughts

There Are No Accidents

I have come to believe that there are no accidents. Certain events and things that happen to us, around us, would make it seem, that there are accidents, but in my thinking these days, I get the strong feeling and truly believe that everything that appears to happen to us in the big dream, must have a purpose. Now it must seem difficult to accept the idea, that when we become ill . . . that could have a purpose, and it also must be difficult to accept, that when we can't pay our rent, that as well, must have a purpose. With the Course, what I've managed to see quite clearly, is that, the learning experiences, are never punishments, as I once believed they were, but are simply opportunities for our ongoing education. That education as I see it, is a series of learning experiences, that keep occurring as we recognize our own desire and readiness to grow. Where and how we are growing is no longer a mystery to me. I believe that we are all in some way, climbing some sort of an invisible ladder and that each and everyone of us is attempting to get back to a place, that we truly have never left, that place being GOD'S House or Heaven, if you prefer. Now the reason I say that we never left, is that as long as we remain in the illusion, the big dream, we actually believe, that in some way we actually could have separated ourselves from GOD, when the truth is, that we never did. Everything that I and everyone else has relearned by our experiences in the illusion are for our benefit and certainly for our own Spiritual growth.

Louise Hay, whose books I used to print, used a marvelous expression which was, 'that we should be the most thankful, to those people who seem to push our buttons the most, because these are the very same people, who will help us to learn, precisely, what it is, we came in to learn'. No, they and you and me are not here by accident, just as you, are not reading this book by accident. There is something that you will see or read in this book, without a doubt, which you already know, but, have momentarily forgotten. The same thing applies to that person that comes into your life, that you feel is not wanted in your life and unless you can turn the fear, of what your ego is telling you that person is there for, your experience will not be a learning experience, but rather a fearful experience. It seems to me

* A Course in Miracles is published by the Foundation For Inner Peace, Glen Ellen, CA.

that every lesson is a lesson in Love and in some way forgiveness. It also seems to me that even when we seem to have bumped into someone, quite by accident, these days, I feel that, no it's not an accident but it is a clear opportunity for learning and maybe a date that had been set up years or centuries ago. Perhaps we have made this date years or centuries ago, for the expressed purpose of rendez-vousing at this particular time, at this particular place, because, we have something to teach each other and we have something to learn from each other. There is something, some reason that we have come together and it seems to point out to me, that the reason is, that there is something we have the need of 'working out'.

A good deal of the Course, relates to relationships. The special love relationship, which sometimes turns quickly into the special hate relationship. Why it spends so much time on relationships is simply because there are no 'accidental relationships'. For those who accept multiple lifetimes, (and the Course indicates, that that is your choice) there just may have been something in a previous lifetime, that you and the other person, still have a need, to work that something out. Metaphysics has taught me, that when we are with someone in any type of relationship in this lifetime, the chances are strong that we have been with that Soul or Spirit in another lifetime. In other words, we know each other and have been together before.

We don't seem to know or even recognize each other in this particular embodiment, but there is a familiarity, a voice perhaps saying to us in our consciousness, we've been together before. Many people I have met claim that they have brought into this life with them, certain illnesses, problems and even complain of paying for the sins of the fathers or their father's fathers, or even their father's father's fathers. Most of us do not carry around with us, any of these ancient memories . . . thank GOD. Can you imagine carrying around the guilt, built up through centuries when we have the enormous pressures we build up, just thinking about and handling the guilt, of this lifetime.

My wife Judy related a story to me years ago, that she tells me her mother told her, when she was a little girl. Judy called it a 'bubermeiser' (yiddish for 'an old wife's tale') but who knows. Anyway the story goes like this. 'Before we are born GOD takes his finger and makes an indentation on our upper lip and that immedi-

---

* A Course in Miracles is published by the Foundation For Inner Peace, Glen Ellen, CA.

ately makes us forget all of the nonsense, garnered in previous lifetimes'.

Dealing with this lifetime, is more than enough, for any of us and getting ourselves into trouble, is not at all difficult for most of us. We seem to have our own special way of going along real well and then suddenly we're up to our necks in deep do do. Getting out of the do do is not always easy and by the same token, not always as quick as we would like it to be, but we can extricate ourselves out of the seeming problems by once again, remembering our true identities and recognizing that these seeming problems are learning experiences, not punishments and that they are definitely not accidents.

My Thoughts

Healing As A Release From Fear

In 1984 I assembled and printed a book entitled, Messages From Our Elder Brother . . Jesus, in which I have taken 'first person' messages from A Course In Miracles. These messages are where Jesus, actually seems to be talking directly to us and while I didn't put all of his messages into the book, my favorites made their way into that work. On page twenty four of my book, I used the quote that appears in the Course on page nineteen of the Text of the Course and I think, it is what probably turned me on to the work I enjoy doing these days, which is Healing thru GOD.

The quote goes like this:

'Our emphasis is now on healing. The miracle is the means, The Atonement is the principle, and healing is the result. To speak of 'a miracle of healing' is to combine two orders of reality inappropriately. Healing is not a miracle. The Atonement, or the final miracle, is a remedy and any type of healing is a result. The kind of error to which Atonement is applied is irrelevant. All healing is essentially, the release from fear. To undertake this you cannot be fearful yourself. You do not understand healing because of your own fear.

The words 'all healing is essentially the release from fear' must be one of the most important lines, in the Course. What it is saying in that single sentence is that, in the illusion, the big dream, our fear, is what is creating the problem and until we can release our fear, the problem, whatever it might appear to be, will not leave. As the Course puts it, we need a miracle, a change of mind, a change in how we are perceiving things, a change from ego thinking, to a change to, Holy Spirit knowledge. We are told, that when we ask Holy Spirit for the miracle, the change, if it is in our and everyone elses involved, best interests, it is always handled and taken care of by the Holy Spirit. This results in what the Course calls the Atonement.

As a kid growing up in the Bronx, I was informed quite early in life, that I was a member of the Jewish faith and that there were certain obligations, that I as a Jewish person, had to conform to. The Ten Commandments led the list, Honoring GOD, Mom and Dad,

*A Course in Miracles is published by the Foundation For Inner Peace, Glen Ellen, CA.

-53-

came second followed by the biggie, not to kill, etc. One of the things most children of the Jewish faith are also taught early in life, is that there is a Holy Day in the Jewish calendar, called Yom Kipor, or translated into English, The Day Of Atonement. Now my understanding of Yom Kipor as a kid and even as an adult, was that this Day Of Atonement was the most important holiday in the Hebrew calendar and the reason for it's importance is, that this is the one day each year, when we go to the Synagogue and take all of our collective sins, ask GOD to forgive us for these collective sins and GOD, hearing us asking for this forgiveness of our sins, suddenly and without any fanfare, forgives us and all of our sins are forgiven. We were instantly absolved of all our sins and would walk out of the Synagogue, minus a great deal of guilt. For many years, I thought that this was the way to go and not only observed, my Jewish customs and traditions, but also practiced these customs and traditions, as well. One thing that bothered me, all of the times I walked to the Synagogue, from my home was that I constantly kept wondering, what sins did I have? What wrongs against GOD, or family, or friends, or anyone, had I committed? Generally, I drew a blank, but continued to go to Synagogue, every Yom Kipor, in order I felt, to stay on GOD'S good side.

When Paul Steinberg and I started the first study group of A Course In Miracles, Paul did a marvelous job in explaining all of the words, terms and applications, but the one word in the Course, that I could never seem to really grasp or understand, was the word Atonement. We are told in the Clarification Of Terms in The Teachers Manual, Book III, of the Course that 'the Atonement is the correction of perception' and 'the means of the Atonement is forgiveness.' I read it, reread it and reread it, but it just didn't penetrate. It wasn't until I started going out and lecturing that Holy Spirit seemed to give me a clearer explanation of the word Atonement and I use it as a way of explaining the process, not the word.

As we mentioned, the word 'miracle' does not appear with a capital 'm', because we learn, it is not of GOD. The word Atonement is always shown with a capital 'A', indicating that it is of GOD. So, what really happens with this miracle? In my lectures, this is the way I have been guided to explain it.

* A Course in Miracles is published by the Foundation For Inner Peace, Glen Ellen, CA.

Have you ever heard or read, where a woman, seeing her child trapped under the wheels of an automobile, suddenly is able to run over to this automobile, take hold of the bumper, and lift the car off of the trapped child and pull the child to safety. I'm sure that all of us have heard or read of such a story and I would guess that most of us would consider this a miracle. Let's explore this story a little more in depth.

Let's visualize a woman, standing on a very busy intersection in a large city, holding her child's hand, when suddenly a man standing behind her, taps her on the shoulder and asks, 'which way is forty-ninth and Broadway? The woman, perhaps a bit startled, lets go of her child's hand, turns around and starts to tell the man how to find the street, he's looking for. With her attention diverted at that moment, the woman does not notice that her child has just dashed in front of an oncoming automobile and is now pinned under this car. The woman turns around, realizing that the child is no longer next to her, looks out into the street, sees her child under the car and screams, 'oh my GOD, Help me.' As the Course would define it, this is 'asking' GOD or the Holy Spirit, or Jesus for the miracle, the correction, of what we think, we are perceiving. What happens next, is, that the woman not at all sure that there is anything that she can actually do, without hesitation, puts one foot off of the curb, and as soon as the other foot comes down in the street, the miracle is starting to happen. She has now gone from a thinking of 'I can't' to with GOD'S Help, 'I Can'. She runs up to the car knowing, not doubting, not fearing, that with GOD'S Help, she will be able to do, whatever needs to be done. She puts her hands on the bumper of the car, knowing that she will succeed and with determination and knowledgeable certainty, lifts the car off of the trapped child and the child is pulled to safety. The whole episode is now done, accomplished . . . the Atonement, has now happened. The Atonement is the result of the miracle or as the Course puts it, It is the correction of perception.

What has occurred is that the woman facing the absolute necessity of helping her child, has forgotten that 'she couldn't' and was reminded and shown, that 'she could'. The very same principals apply to all of us when we ask for the miracle and there are absolutely no limits, as to what miracles, will be answered, with the

Atonement. In the Text, Book I, Page 1, we are given by Jesus and the Holy Spirit 'THE MEANING OF MIRACLES', which are 50 Principals Of Miracles. Number one principle in the fifty principals is . . .

1. There is no order of difficulty in miracles. One is not 'harder' or 'bigger' than another. They are all the same.
All expressions of love are maximal.

Now if this principle is true and at this point in my life, I believe it is, then what this principal is also encompassing, is, that there is also no difficulty in healing. That no illness presents a greater problem to us, than another. To say it another way, AIDS or Cancer, is no more difficult to heal, than is a cold, a sore throat or even a pimple on our nose. If there is no order of difficulty, there cannot be an order of difficulty in healing.

This is our moment of truth . . . Until your mind accepts this as Truth and we're definitely talking about our GOD Mind, not our ego mind, just as soon as this becomes your truth, and you ask for the miracle, you are guaranteed, the Atonement, and will receive healing.

You see . . . it is the release from fear . . . and the mind has gone from a place of chaos . . . to a place of peacefulness.

* Text, Book I of A Course in Miracles, is published by the Foundation For Inner Peace, Glen Ellen, CA.

Your Only Goal Should Be The Peace Of GOD

According to the Course, listening to the ego brings chaos and disaster, while listening to The GOD Mind brings only Peace and Joy. We are also introduced to a word, which sounds kind of sexist, but the word encompasses every last one of us, without exception. The word I'm referring to is Sonship. The Sonship embodies every single one of your brothers, every single one of your sisters and even Jesus is considered a part of the Sonship. Notice that the word is capital 'S', which as I've explained, means that the entire sum total of us, yes every single last one of us represent and comprise, the Sonship. Throughout my life, before my introduction to the Course, a good deal of my time was spent, planning, plotting, and goal setting. I had this idea, this belief, that in order to have what you would need in the future, you should plan now, so that as your birthdays kept passing, you would have everything needed and want for nothing in your old age, if you lived to an old age. Goal setting, was the only way, I believed I, or anyone else, could achieve having everything that I would need, for a bright happy future. This feeling or belief if you prefer, stayed with me, even some years, after my introduction to the Course. I'm pleased to say, that right now, I have for the most part, if not completely, given up goal setting and concentrate more, on living in the now.

I want to share a true story, with you, that helped me to see the Wisdom, in making the Peace of GOD, my only goal. During the time I was turning out book after book, which were the years of 1977 thru 1987, I had a friend who read everything, I printed or published. When this friend would call, his first question would always be, what new book are you working on and when will it be finished? He would pester me to let him read the galley proofs, before I could even print and bind, because waiting for the completion of a book, was not for him. I figured that my friend must be on a Spiritual search and that since he was a millionaire and was in excellent health, his life had to be working. As far as I can remember, I can't recall his ever buying a book from me, which I'm certain, bothered me in those days, but never the less, every time I saw my friend, he would walk off with my latest published effort. I even gave him a set of the Course and invited him to our Course meetings. I don't recall him

* *A Course in Miracles is published by the Foundation For Inner Peace, Glen Ellen, CA.*

ever showing up at our Tuesday night meetings, or discussing the Course with me but we spent long hours talking about metaphysics, and living in the Bronx. We met often during my years on Long Island and would even get together socially and I thought I got to know my friend, real well.

One day he called me, asked if I would be at my office and whether he could see me' on a matter of utmost urgency. I picked up on his anger, and upset and invited him to come over to my office. An hour later, he was sitting with me and in great pain said, 'my partner, is stealing from me.' I looked at my friend, not believing what I had just heard and replied, 'no way.' I knew his partner, almost as well as I knew my friend and there was not the slightest chance, as far as I was concerned, that my friend's partner could or would steal from my friend. I responded to my friends accusation, reminded him that I knew his partner and that it just couldn't be true. I advised him to lighten up and if he had any suspicions, to talk to his partner in a loving way. I said, that even if his fears were true, this was a learning experience for both partners and the only answer, according to everything that I knew at that time, was forgiveness . . . not attack. He looked at me and in a very angry, defiant tone said, 'I'm going to send my partner to jail and get back all of the money he stole from me.' I looked at my friend, saw his pain and urged, just have a talk with your partner, don't put you or him, thru this pain. It can only result in more pain and suffering for both of you and nobody but the attorneys, will be the winners. Stubbornly, my friend said; I'm going to get my partner, if it takes the rest of my life and I don't care, what it costs. I argued, using one of my favorite lines from the Course, 'would you rather be right, or happy?' He didn't hear me and regrettably, he left my office, angrier than when he had walked in.

During the next several years, the visits from my friend were still continuing and true to his words, he did break off his business relationship with his partner and started court proceedings. Strangely enough, his partner wound up with all of the employees, in a new office location and from what I had heard, was doing very well. My friend on the other hand took a shot at a new business, same line and failed, tried again, failed again. Throughout the time my friend started court proceedings, in order to 'break his former partner,' my

---

* A Course in Miracles is published by the Foundation For Inner Peace, Glen Ellen, CA.

friend's fortunes were rapidly disappearing and one day at one of our visits, he confessed to me that he was broke and that the only thing he had left was his house and that even the house was getting to expensive to keep. He was completely baffled by the whole experience and still wasn't right . . . wasn't happy. Totally bewildered by the entire experience, as we sat together that day, he introduced a new fear, a new accusation. This time, my dear friend said that now, his son, had also betrayed him, stolen from him and that in his thinking, he no longer had a son. I listened and felt great compassion for this very confused friend of mine, who had at one time, not that many years ago, seemed to have it all, by the world's standards and now was in appearance, broken, and soon to be, according to him, destitute. For the first time in his life, he had a genuine fear of not being able to outlive, his money and as I listened to him, I reminded him that he still had his health but that I believed, he was definitely placing his health in serious jeopardy and that he should stop all of this attack and forgive. He reprimanded me, left my office and I didn't see him again, for about a year.

The telephone rang and I was delighted to hear my friend's voice on the other end. After sharing with me some of the things going on in his life, he asked if he could come over to the office, because he had news of a very exciting nature and couldn't wait to share it with me. An hour later we were sitting together, just like old times, I noticed his hair was a little grayer and he had lost some weight but over all he looked well and I asked, 'what's this exciting news, you want to share with me?' He looked straight into my eyes replied without any hesitation, 'Saul, this morning, I came up with a fantastic five year goal. It came to me, while I was shaving and I've got it all down on paper. It's going to get me back all of the monies and possessions I've lost and this set of goals, will put me right back on top, once I put them into work'. As we sat there in my office, he elaborated detail after detail about his five year goals and I listened to each one of his goals and throughout his sharing his new found goal plan, he kept talking about getting even with his former partner, his son and everyone of his former employees, as well as his former customers. He predicted that all of his millions would be back, without fail, precisely in five years and that setting these goals, was the only way it could, or would, happen. I listened to my friend, patiently and lovingly, trying my best, not to be judgmental and as I sat hearing this dear friend sharing his dream with me, I couldn't help but think, 'he just doesn't understand'.

Finally, after about an hour of his sharing his goals and their expected results, he asked, 'Well Saul, what do you think?' I looked at my friend and asked, 'how do you feel, right now, this second?' He looked at me, surprised that I had answered his question with my question and he asked, 'what do you mean?' I answered, and asked once again, 'how do you feel, right now, this second, sitting here in my office, how do you feel right now?' He thought about my question for just a moment and shot back, 'I feel like shit.' With his admission that he felt terrible, I asked him if it would not be better for him to feel good, right now, rather than to be concerning himself about five years, from now. Would it not be better for you, I asked, to get yourself back to a place of Peace, than remaining in this place of chaotic fearful thinking, that could, in my opinion, only guarantee more and greater problems, in his future. I tried to explain that in order for his life to reach any kind of a happy time period, he must start right now, this moment, to totally let go of the past and to try and see the Light in each and everyone of the people he was condemning.

He half listened but left my office that day, determined that his five year goals, were the one and only answer to rescue him from him 'seeming' problems and I didn't hear anything from him or about him, for about a year.

The next news I heard about my friend, was that he had experienced a severe heart attack and I went to visit him in the hospital. Despite all of my wonderful material, that he had read, listened to and watched on his VCR, here he was lying in a hospital bed, all kind of tubes attached to his body, still feeling like shit, as he put it and he was still putting the blame, the responsibility, on someone else. As I think about that visit to the hospital, I am reminded of what has become for me, a most important quote from the Course. It is . . .

*A Course in Miracles is published by the Foundation For Inner Peace, Glen Ellen, CA.

'I am responsible for what I see.
I choose the feelings I experience,
and I decide upon the goal I would achieve.
And everything that seems to happen to me
I ask for, and receive as I have asked.'

This is without a doubt, just one of the major lessons, each and everyone of us, has come into whatever bodies, we have chosen, to learn. That we must take responsibility, for everything, without exception, that seems to go on with us. We also should focus, totally in the 'now', because 'now', is the only time there is. We have absolutely no ability to relive or undo the past nor do we have any idea of what is in the future. Sure we have many Psychics that seem to have an ability to predict the future. I've printed books for some of them, but are they correct in their predictions, one hundred percent of the time? I doubt it. Living in the 'now', and only in the 'now', seems to be the answer. This is the time, the only time, to be happy. We need to make each and every moment, each and every minute, each and every hour, each and every day and each and every year, peaceful and as a result, happy. Living totally in the 'now', is the only way, that peace of Mind, Inner Peace, can happen. That should be, our one and only goal.

---

*A Course in Miracles is published by the Foundation For Inner Peace, Glen Ellen, CA.

My Thoughts

One Person Can Make A Difference

Recently I did a lecture at an Attitudinal Healing Center in a town called Winter Park, located a few miles east of Orlando, here in Florida. This Center called The Loren Quinn Institute describes itself as:

'A Center for Personal Growth and Healing Through Attitudinal Change'

This month, The Loren Quinn Institute is celebrating its first anniversary and in its Statement of Purpose, it states that they wish

To provide an environment where our essential unity with the Creator and one another can be experienced.

To provide a learning center for individual and collective development which affirms that Truth is available to all through beneficent inner guidance.

To offer safe and supported spaces, where persons can join with others to experience at their own pace and of their own volition, how specific attitudinal change can result in more joyful and harmonious living.

To develop a resource center of materials and activities which facilitates the healing experience of inner peace.

The Loren Quinn Institute is not the first or only Attitudinal Healing Center in our country, there are many others. Almost every state I lecture in seems to have their own Center and if they don't, I am always approached, after doing a session on Attitudinal Healing, by someone, who has been sent by GOD, to perhaps start a Center in their town.

The first Attitudinal Healing Center in this country was the Center For Attitudinal Healing, located in a tiny little town called Tiburon, located just across the bay from San Francisco, in California. This Center, the world's very first Center, was founded by a man, who was in great need at that time of serving GOD and all of his brothers and sisters, without exception. The man I'm referring to of course has seen great change occur in this world, in this country and most certainly, in his own life, since 1975. The man I'm referring to is of course, Gerald G. Jampolsky, M.D. and I've known Dr. Jampolsky since that time.

I guess what captivated the imaginations of many people, including me, was a brand new concept that Dr. Jampolsky brought forward and ran with. That concept started with Gerry's introduction to the Course, at a time when he was in great need of Peace and Healing, in his own life and what he started, has become the focus, for so many, many people, wishing, hoping, daring to summon the courage, to Heal through GOD. As mentioned, Gerry himself had this great need of Healing and as he has said many times, for perhaps the first time, in his life, he heard an inner voice say, physician Heal thyself. His studies of the Course took him on a new journey and certainly a new way of seeing things. He was guided to change the way he was practicing medicine, and introduced to the world a brand new concept, conceived out of his studies of the Course and he was on his way, not only towards his own Healing, but also affecting the lives and experiences of many others.

Gerry was guided to work with children who were terminally ill, and according to their doctors, had little or no chance of survival. In those days, for most people, a doctor telling you that the child or adult had only so much time left, didn't leave one, couldn't leave one, with a whole lot of hope. Gerry was guided to change that, and did. For the first time, as far as I know, a medical doctor volunteered to work with children, whose doctors had told the parents that there was no hope and that their children would die . . . and, there was nothing further that could be done.

Gerry was guided to offer his services as a doctor to these terminally ill children, with a brand new concept. The concept was and is Attitudinal Healing, a brand new therapy, not using the traditional medical methods, but introducing a brand new idea, that sickness, all sickness, is of the mind and since all sickness is of the mind, only the GOD Mind can eliminate the 'supposed' problem.

I remember watching Gerry on some of TV's most popular shows and the host's always seemed so baffled by Gerry's theories

*A Course in Miracles is published by the Foundation For Inner Peace, Glen Ellen, CA.

and beliefs but the crazy thing was, that Gerry's methods were working. Children who were supposed to be dead, were living and in some cases, terminal diseases, were disappearing. The world was suddenly receiving a message from GOD, Jesus and the Holy Spirit, that there was no need to be sick and no reason to die. The whole idea, the whole concept was something that we made up. The reason that some of these kids were living and not dying was simply, that they changed their minds. Gerry's fame grew and Gerry's life changed, very much for the better. He started to meet people, who also were intrigued with this brand new concept of Attitudinal Healing and they started to perceive, that perhaps . . . this stuff, could work and it did. In Gerry's book, One Person Can Make A Difference, Gerry's sub title is 'Ordinary People Doing Extraordinary Things' and it is Gerry's accounting of nine different people telling their stories about how they went from a place of guilt, doubt and fear, to a place of inner peace, through GOD. Gerry Jampolsky has written several books which have become the Bibles of Attitudinal Healing and has been an inspiration and surely is one person, who did make a difference for hundreds of thousands of people all over the world . . . including me. The second doctor, who I feel has made a tremendous difference and that I want to talk about, is a man that I met way back in 1978, whose name is David R. Hawkins, M.D.

The first time I set eyes on Dave Hawkins, he greeted me with the words, 'how do you do Mr. Steinberg, my name is David R. Hawkins, I'm a physician and I'm dying. I've heard that you have a set of books entitled A Course In Miracles. Do you think they can help me?' I looked at this very thin man standing in front of me and I replied, 'that's up to you.' I offered him a seat and we started to talk about what he saw as his problems and his inability to help his step daughter out of her terminal illness and the fact that he had manifested twenty one life threatening illnesses, into his own life. He was convinced, I believe, at that time, that he did not have very much more time, to spend on this planet. As he left my office that day, a set of A Course In Miracles, tucked under his arm, my belief at that moment was that I'd probably never see him again. I was wrong. A week later he was back and after another short conversation, this time he left with four sets of the Course under his arm. The following week, Dave was back and this time asked me for eight sets of the

* A Course in Miracles is published by the Foundation For Inner Peace, Glen Ellen, CA.
* Dr. Gerald G. Jampolsky is published by Bantem Books, NY, and Celestral Arts, CA.

Course and I wondered what he was going to do, with eight sets of A Course In Miracles. I remember carrying down the sets to his car, because he didn't have the strength to do so himself. The next week Dave Hawkins came back and asked me to give him sixteen sets and as I carried the sixteen sets down to his car, I figured that he must be eating the books, for strength and energy, to help to combat his twenty one life threatening illnesses. The following week Dave was back in my office, this time asking me for thirty two sets of the Course and I was bursting with curiosity to find out what he was doing with all of these books. I put the thirty two sets on a hand cart, accompanied Dave down to his car and placed the cases into his trunk and finally asked Dave what he was doing with all of these sets of the Course. He looked at me and said 'Saul, I am giving these books to every physician I know. I believe that this material is the true answer to Healing and I believe that it should be mandatory, that every physician, before he or she is allowed to graduate Medical School, should be made to study A Course In Miracles'. Further he said, 'it also should be mandatory, that no patient should be allowed into a doctor's office, until they have studied the Course and finally, that no one should be accepted, or registered into a hospital, unless they have studied the Course.'

Wow, I thought, I had never heard anyone talk like this, nor had I ever heard a doctor, an M D., voice such an opinion. David Hawkins, joined our A Course In Miracles group soon after and he started to 'lose' his illnesses, one after another. He was so thankful, that he donated space to us, in a hospital that he owned and operated, and the second Attitudinal Healing Center was born. Dave Hawkins put his hand in his pocket and flew Gerry Jampolsky and some of Gerry's staff from the Center in Tiburon, to Long Island and a group of more than a hundred people gathered in Dave's home for a three day intensive on how to run an Attitudinal Healing Center. It was a very powerful weekend for everyone of us and Gerry's love, expertise and experience was felt by all. Our Center was off and running way back in the late seventies and none of us could imagine what was planned for us.

In a short time, Dave Hawkins, with the help of the Holy Spirit, Jesus, A Course In Miracles and the Psychotherapy Booklet, had no more trace of any of the twenty one life threatening illnesses and he

* A Course in Miracles and Psycotherapy, Purpose, Process and Practice are published by the Foundation For Inner Peace, Glen Ellen, CA.

gave up all of his material things and moved to a place called Sedona, located in the beautiful state of Arizona. I lost touch with David until we did a lecture together in Detroit, Michigan in 1983. When I saw him for the first time in Detroit I was amazed that his appearance was completely different and he looked to me, to be the picture of health . . . . and he was. I also noticed that he wasn't wearing his eyeglasses and asked, 'Dave, where are your glasses?' He smiled and said, 'Saul, I no longer wear glasses.' Feeling a bit puzzled by his response, I then asked 'how did you accomplish that?' Dave looked at me and said, 'Saul, you were the one that showed me how.' I understood and right after that weekend, for the first time in many years, I removed my glasses and found no further need for them.

A few years later while flying back from a video show I had attended, I was staring out of the window of the plane and suddenly without warning, I started to see an image of words, rolling in a downward motion, and the words were not something I had been thinking about at that moment but were a listing in a specific sequence. The sequence was . . .

1. Stress
2. Weight
3. Alcoholism
4. Illness
5. Spiritual First Aid
6. Depression
7. Pain and Suffering
8. Health
19. Sex
10. Worry, Fear and Anxiety
11. The Aging Process
12. Handling Major Crisis

I had no idea what I was seeing in that image but I took out my pen and wrote down the twelve terms I saw and wondered, what they meant. I closed my eyes and started to meditate and soon it was clear to me that I was being guided to put out a series of videos that would clarify some of the Attitudinal Healing Concepts given to Gerry Jampolsky and these same concepts that Dave Hawkins had used in his own Healing through GOD. A vision of Dave Hawkins came into my thoughts and I knew that I was to call Dave, the following day. I reviewed the 12 different problems that Spirit had just given me and came up with a title called 12 Office Visits With The Good Doctor. The following day, I called Dave Hawkins, told him about my vision and mentioned that he was the man, Holy Spirit wanted for the series of videos and asked if he would do it. His reply to me was, 'Saul it sounds right but I must ask Spirit if I should do it.' I completely understood and asked Dave to call me as soon as he got his answer.

* 12 Office Visits With The Good Doctor, Mind and Miracles, Ft. Lauderdale, FL.

The next day he called back and said that Holy Spirit had given him a green light and asked when I wanted to start. In less than three months, we had completed 12 Office Visits With The Good Doctor and I have no idea, how many people they have helped, but I know quite a few, who have reversed their illnesses, using these tapes as a guide.

The following year Spirit once again spoke to me and suggested that we do another series, which we appropriately named The Sedona Series. This is a series of four videos dealing with four of the most dreaded diseases . . .

1. Cancer   3. Cardiovascular Problems
2. AIDS   4. Drug and Alcohol Addictions

These video tapes were completed even quicker than the Twelve Office Visits With The Good Doctor and suddenly Holy Spirit had given to the world, sixteen Attitudinal Healing video tapes, compliments of Dr. David R. Hawkins and myself. Once again, it was shown that One Person Can Make A Difference.

The last man I want to tell you about, also has provided and made a difference, that man, another doctor, another very dear friend, Dr. Jasper B. Becker. Jappy, as he prefers to be called, is the man along with his wife Cathy, that started The Loren Quinn Institute in Winter Park, Florida, mentioned at the beginning of this chapter.

I first met Jappy and Cathy at a Forgiveness Workshop that we were doing in Orlando, several years ago. Both Cathy and Jappy were very distraught at that time due to their daughter Loren's leaving her body in a most tragic automobile 'accident.' One can imagine their pain and their grief to see this young beautiful child, leaving her body, so early in her life. I suspect that they came to that lecture that weekend in Orlando, to ascertain whether or not Forgiveness of the young man who was driving the other automobile, could in any way help to alleviate, their pain. Apparently they accepted some, or perhaps most of the Course's wisdom dealing with Forgiveness and when we did one of our Miracle Jamborees in Daytona Beach, as we do each year, both Cathy and Jappy were there and they asked about Attitudinal Healing. I told them many things and as my memory reminds me now, I sent them a book entitled

* *The Sedona Series, Mind and Miracles, Ft. Lauderdale, FL.*

Attitudinal Healing A Guide For Groups and Individuals, written by a wonderful lady by the name of Genevieve Weirich. Now Jappy at that time was practicing Urology, was quite busy with his practice and it never occurred to me that he would consider giving up a lucrative medical practice, to involve himself in Attitudinal Healing but that is precisely what happened. In August of 1991, Jappy and Cathy Becker opened the doors of The Loren Quinn Institute, in Winter Park, Florida. Here is a physician with twenty five years of Urology experience under his belt and he's giving up what most people would see as 'the good life' and volunteering to spend the rest of his time with and in, Attitudinal Healing, offering Healing through attitudinal change to people experiencing life-threatening illness, who find themselves in crisis, totally without charge.

Jap Becker is using the concept originated and popularized by Gerry Jampolsky and feels, in Attitudinal Healing, we define health as 'Inner Peace' and says, 'when one is peaceful, he or she, is far better able to cope with their problems and respond to true Healing.' Dr. Becker's Center, The Loren Quinn Institute, is currently providing a Lighthouse, guided by a beacon of Light . . . to many in the area. The three men I have just told you about are wonderful examples of individuals who most certainly have made a profound difference in all of our lives. The Course explains to us that when we do something for someone else, we are literally doing whatever we're doing, for the entire Sonship and reap the benefits as well.

Start thinking of yourself, as one person, who can make a difference. You are, you know.

---

* *Attitudinal Healing, A Guide For Groups and Individuals, by Genevieve Werrich, Cambridge Publishing, Grand Rapids, MI.*
* *Distributed by Mind and Miracles, Ft. Lauderdale, FL.*

My Thoughts

Do Any Of Us Go To Heaven?

In a section of the Text, Page 249, we are told by Jesus and the Holy Spirit that 'GOD wills you be in Heaven, and nothing can keep you from it, or it from you. Your wildest misperceptions, your weird imaginings, your blackest nightmares all mean nothing' and then it goes on to say, 'They will not prevail against the peace GOD wills for you.'

I'm sure that the above comes as news to a great many of us. You can't put on a radio on Sunday, or turn on your TV and not hear some person, blasting us with the threat that GOD is going to get us and we are going straight to hell. The messages are usually the same, regardless of who is giving us the message. We're told that Jesus, paid with his life, for our sins, and that we're most certainly going to hell, if we don't change our ways, repent, recognize Jesus as our only savior and mail in a few bucks, to insure that we will be forgiven, for all of our collective sins.

Many years ago, I don't know exactly when, but let's say it was at a time, when my understanding of the Course, was just starting to come, I felt the need to start practicing this concept the Course, spoke so much about, the concept of Forgiveness. The first person I thought about, that I figured needed Forgiveness was Hitler, because in my thinking at that time I figured that he was the cause of unhappiness for more people, than perhaps, anyone in history. Try as I did, I found it totally impossible, to think about Adolph Hitler, without despising him. Everytime I would try to picture him surrounded by Light, I would immediately feel my ego mind kick in and a picture of a concentration camp would suddenly appear in my thinking and immediately with that horror in mind, I would give up on trying to see Adolph Hitler, in the Light.

What turned that whole thing around for me, was, that Holy Spirit lovingly guided me to become aware that the Forgiveness that I was trying to muster for Adolph, was not for Adolph at all . . . it was for me. I suddenly understood that when we hold on to a grievance, any grievance, where we hold someone else responsible for our pain, we will stay in and with that pain, for as long as we choose. Even if the person we think dealt us the pain, that we are

* Pg. 249, Text of A Course in Miracles is published by the Foundation For Inner Peace, Glen Ellen, CA.

holding on to, is dead and buried, we can still be walking around with that pain, fifty or sixty years later. The more I understand this concept, so beautifully explained in the Course, the more I am able to utilize it in my own life, in my own experience.

At one of our Miracle Jamborees, held a few years ago, the topic was Forgiveness and at the last session on the Sunday, we ask whomever chooses to stand up and share, to share, whatever they choose to share. A woman perhaps in her mid seventies, stood up and said that she had been in pain for the past sixty seven years and that it was only that morning after experiencing Bo Abernethy's Light workshop, based on going within and finding it within yourself, to Forgive, that she was finding Peace, at last. She related to all in attendance, that as a little girl, she was sexually attacked by an uncle that she loved and trusted very much and that the pain of that experience stayed with her all these years. She went on to say, that she loved this uncle so very much, that it actually manifested a great deal of guilt for her to think of this man, in an unloving way. Just imagine if you will, carrying around all this pain for so many years. As I listened to this dear lady, I saw her carrying a huge bag of stone, her body sagging under the weight of all that stone, dragging it and herself, day after day, year after year, with the only release, from all this pressure, being able to Forgive, her long gone Uncle. Here she was, telling all of us, that she was at last, Peaceful.

Now, most of us hearing or reading about a horror story like this, would most certainly think and feel that we should get the bastard, string him up by the neck, until the punishment we are meaning to inflict, is carried out. Surely in this world's opinion, this is justice, and all crime should be punished, with justice being doled out, befitting the crime. Most people would also feel that the 'sin' committed, is most definitely, committed against GOD, and that GOD will get us for the sin, sooner or later. We start to live our lives, waiting for GOD'S imaginary ax to fall and some of us start to think we should hurry up the punishment and leave the body, sooner than we need to. This can be accomplished in many different ways, thru illness, depression, pain and suffering and suicide, which is really a combination of the four ego actions mentioned.

There have been many experiences that I personally have been given by the Holy Spirit, in my life up to this point that have been 'doozies' as the world might perceive them to be. I can recall a three hundred and fifty pound man coming into my office, while on Long Island, and threatening to break some of my bones, if I didn't pay the interest, he felt was due, since I was late in paying the full amount of money I owed on an oil bill. Then there was another time that a man took a thirteen inch knife, held it to my throat and threatened to drive it through my neck if I didn't come up with the monies I owed on some negative and plate work he had done for me. One would ask, what did these people have going on in their minds, that they could actually get themselves worked up to such a frenzy, that they could want to commit violence, to a brother or sister. What I've concluded is that the person committing the crime is frightened out of his or her wits and the fear has so consumed that person's thinking, that they become totally unrational. In the case of the two men I mentioned, somehow as the threats were going on, I did what the Course suggests we should do, and that is to try at the very moment you are confronted with the threat, you should try to see the Christ in that brother or sister and offer to them Love . . . instead of fear. While this concept must seem very strange to most of us, it's the only thing that works. Recognize if something that you find uncomfortable is occurring to you, it is a learning/growing experience, that you yourself are in need of, for your own Spiritual growth. Try to face the experience without fear, offering Love and compassion to the brother or sister who seems to be administering the pain to you and through this Forgiveness process we are talking about, the whole episode results in your being Peaceful, as opposed to your feeling attacked and being the 'victim'. We can only be a 'victim', if we allow ourselves to be a 'victim'.

Heaven, as noted earlier, is guaranteed to each and everyone of us, without exception. Another of the most asked questions we get asked at our lectures, is:

'Are we all going to Heaven, or are some of us headed in a totally different direction?'

The Course teaches us, that indeed, we are all going to Heaven, and only to Heaven. It gently reminds us that none of us go . . . until we all go. We all go en masse only when each and every one of us, without exception, can see the Christ, the Light, in each and every

* A Course in Miracles is published by the Foundation For Inner Peace, Glen Ellen, CA.

one of us, also without exception. It is at that point, that all of us will be practicing the concept that all of this is teaching . . . that concept being 'Unconditional Love'. Until we know with knowledgeable certainty, that each and everyone of us is perfect, none of us get to Heaven.

Paul Steinberg gave me the best analogy, I've ever heard to understand this concept. He said:

> *'Picture each and everyone of us, existing in the world of form, standing a top of a huge flat cliff, each of us by this time have been able to see the Christ, in each and every one of our brothers and sisters, totally without exception and every single last one of us is practicing Unconditional Love. At that time, whenever that time is, and it could be tomorrow, next week, next month or ten thousand years from now, no one knows, but at precisely that moment, when we've all got it, we join hands take a mighty leap off the cliff and the world of form as we know it, no longer exists. We are back in our Fathers House (Heaven) asleep as little children, knowing our 'True Identity'.*

Take heart . . . it's happening, we're all every single one of us . . . on the journey, together.

Peace and Happiness

Not long ago I printed a book entitled, The New Age Guide To Peace and Happiness, Through A Course In Miracles. It was written by another student of the Course, by the name of Marlies a Marca who comes to us by way of Switzerland. I first met Marlies some years ago when I maintained an office in Thousand Oaks, California and I remember with great joy, the first day she walked into my office and said to me, 'Mr. Steinberg, my name is Marlies a Marca, I'm a student of A Course In Miracles, and I want you to publish and print my book. I looked at her and said, that's what I'm here for, let me take a look at the manuscript, and I'll read it. She looked at me and said, well . . . there's a slight problem. I inquired, 'and what might that be?' Cheerfully, she replied, 'well, it's not written yet.' I watched her smile and understood that while perhaps, she had not committed her thoughts to paper, nevertheless, her book was most certainly in her head, and that when she was ready with it on paper, I was the one to publish and print it. I invited her to lunch and we went across the street and proceeded to enjoy a two hour lunch and then spent the rest of that day together.

We discussed many things that day including her work, which was counseling, her vocation which was Attitudinal Healing and her dreams of helping as many people as she possibly could, through her skills as a doctor, and her knowledge of the Course and Course Psychotherapy, which was her concern. When we parted that day, I advised her to try and put some of the things she wanted to say on paper and to try on a daily basis to fastidiously try for a page, a day. I didn't see or hear from Marlies for about five years and by this time I was living in Florida and one day the telephone rang and on the other end of the line I heard this joy filled voice say, 'hi Saul, this is Marlies. I tried to remember who Marlies was, but drew a blank. I asked, 'can you remind me how we know each other?' She replied, 'I'm the gal who asked you to print her book, out in California, but at the time, I had not yet written it. Instantly, I did remember and asked her to send the manuscript to me and when it arrived, I read it and could not put it down.

I would like to share a page or so from Marlies' book and see

---

* The New Age Guide To Peace and Happiness, Through A Course in Miracles, published by Mind and Miracles, Ft. Lauderdale, FL.
* A Course In Miracles is published by the Foundation For Inner Peace, Glen Ellen, CA.

if you don't agree, that these particular thoughts, appearing in Chapter 6 discussing Invulnerability and Forgiveness, are two of the concepts, we all are trying to deal With, every moment of our lives.

INVULNERABILITY AND FORGIVENESS

'Your capability to manifest and make your wishes come true depends on only one thing: your Forgiveness. My son at age 16, was what they call an 'obnoxious nerd', a loner, withdrawn, friendless and angry. I was the main recipient of his anger and it hurt a lot. First I wanted to solve this problem by shipping him off to Switzerland, to live with his father. But he didn't want to go.

Then I started practicing Forgiveness. I started to ignore his verbal abuse. At first it hurt so much sometimes that after it was over, I had to go into my bedroom and cry. After a while of ignoring his negative behavior I hurt less, could sit there and think: 'Here we go again' and just let him rant and rave until he was through and then say: 'Let's go to a movie' or 'What do you want for dinner tonight?' After some confusion on his part, this usually snapped him out of his bad, aggressive mood. I did the FORGIVENESS EXERCISE every night And low and behold, this son of mine transformed right in front of my eyes within three months time He became a friend, a delight to live with, popular, beautiful and open minded All our friends noticed the remarkable change.

'FORGIVENESS OFFERS EVERYTHING I WANT.'

Do you want to receive Enlightenment? Do you want a peaceful, beautiful world? Do you want to feel safe and secure? Do you want to feel invulnerable? Do you want to be loved and cherished by everyone? Forgiveness offers all this to you and more.   Forgiveness is the key to Happiness! This chapter will show you how it is done. First, we have to look at our beliefs. As we believe, so do we perceive. We believe that the world is a dangerous place, that we are vulnerable and that therefore we have to constantly be on guard and careful. We believe we must defend against or attack what we consider evil or dangerous. Therefore, we operate on the basis of FEAR. Our principal motivator is the fear of punishment. And in our interaction with others, we constantly think in terms of defending or attacking.

---

* *A Course in Miracles, Book II, Workbook ACIM, Lesson 34, published by the Foundation For Inner Peace, Glen Ellen, CA.*

J. C. Pearce author of Exploring the Crack in the Cosmic Egg Pocket Books, Gulf and Western Corporation: New York, 1974 Pg. 12, states 'that from childhood, we learn to think along certain culturally limited and defined lines, generally agreed upon through an acculturation process he calls 'metaprogramming' In other words, as a child, certain beliefs are programmed into us by parents, teachers and other adults. These beliefs or these 'metaprograms' say in essence: You better be careful and watch out. There are many, many bad things in 'the world out there' that can happen to you, even if you are good. Pearce says that 'this metaprogram' is an abstract semantic construct based not on reality interaction but on FEAR of reality (author's emphasis) . . Culture arises from and rests squarely on what I call a 'death concept'. This is a notion resulting from reflections on death and in a belief in a universal 'hostility' toward life.' The basic assumption (belief) that the universe is hostile to life creates our negative view of the world and a hostile reality, because as we believe, so do we perceive.'

A Course In Miracles says the same: 'You operate from the belief that you must protect yourself from what is happening because it must contain what threatens you' . . . the world is based on this insane belief. And all its structures, all its thoughts and doubts, penalties and heavy armaments, its legal definitions and its codes, its ethics and its leaders and its gods, all serve but to preserve its sense of threat. For no one who walks the world in armature but must have terror striking at his heart.'

INVULNERABILITY is the result of the belief in the   benevolence of the world, in love and peace, and that therefore nothing can harm me. This positive belief is the exact opposite from the foregoing one, that the world is full of danger. (In Chapter 4, The Theory of Everything, I explained that problems are solved by switching from one polarity to the exact opposite.) INVULNERABILITY means to think no fearful thoughts, to feel no fear and to experience no harm or threat of any kind, neither emotional, nor physical. INVULNERABILITY means to perceive and experience yourself as safe from disasters of all kinds, healthy and happy, and immune to attack from others.'

Marlie's book is filled with many, many wonderful guides to Peace and Happiness and with her experience in working with pain

---

* A Course in Miracles is published by the Foundation For Inner Peace, Glen Ellen, CA.

control, biofeedback, hospices, mental wards, counseling centers, disease and A Course In Miracles, she has taken what has worked for her and her patients and has developed what she calls her 'Theory of Everything', a problem-solving method based on universal principles, that work.

Love, Peace and Happiness is what we all are striving for. If you are not enjoying all three . . . change your mind right now.

* A Course in Miracles is published by the Foundation For Inner Peace, Glen Ellen, CA.
* The New Age Guide To Peace and Happiness is published by Mind and Miracles, Ft. Lauderdale, FL.

I Am Responsible

One of the toughest concepts in the Course, that I had trouble with was this idea that 'everything that seems to happen to me, I have asked for and receive as I have asked.' This is a very frightening thought. If you accept this thought, there is no longer anyone that you can blame for your misfortunes. If you get sick, you can't blame GOD. If you are heavy, you can't blame Mom or Dad. If you are broke, you can't blame the world and if you are unhappy . . . what this means is that you have to take the responsibility, for your unhappiness. Wow . . . what a horrible thought, or, as Riley used to say, 'what a revolting development, this is'.

On page 418 of the Text we are told that 'it is impossible the Son of GOD be merely driven by events outside of him.' Followed by 'It's impossible that happenings that come to him were not his choice.' This clearly is backing up the concept of I Am Responsible. It's so much easier to place the blame on something or someone else when we find ourselves in a situation, that we don't understand and all of us in this world of form, seem to take the easy road out of taking responsibility.

Ever notice, when someone is given bad news by their doctor, the scenario might go something like this:

Mrs. Jones, I'm sorry to say, I have bad news for you. Your tests show that you have Cancer and the prognosis does not look very good. On hearing what Mrs. Jones, immediately, might be accepting, as an automatic death sentence, Mrs. Jones might put her hands up to her head, automatically, lift her head towards the sky and say, 'Oh GOD, what did I do, to deserve this?' The implication and possibly the belief is, this dreaded illness is being given to Mrs. Jones, because of something terrible, that she has done. She tries to think of some sin that she has committed in the past and sometimes, if we can't come up with a reason that GOD is punishing us, we have our families or even our grandparents, or great grandparents, to place, the blame on. We even in some cases, accept that GOD is punishing us for some infraction of our religious beliefs, which we feel we have not observed or followed. Some of our more orthodox religious beliefs, were, I believe, extremely important in their day, to help us learn concepts that would be very helpful to us, but clearly

* Text, Book I, A Course in Miracles is published by the Foundation For Inner Peace, Glen Ellen, CA.

in todays spiritual/psychological world, feeling guilty or believing that GOD is out to get us for non observance of some of our ancient beliefs, has in my opinion, seen it's better days. My study of the Course has re-educated my thinking to feel positively that regardless of what infraction we make, regarding our old beliefs, traditions and customs, lead us to feelings of guilt, doubt and fear. Somehow or another, even with the most advanced thinkers, we are so ingrained with this belief, that GOD will get us, if we break the rules, we're going to get zapped, with all kinds of horrible things.

The Course teaches us that if we have been blaming GOD for anything that seems to be happening to us, we need to address whatever that seems to be, see it as a learning experience, allow our ego mind to make the 'shift' and show 'a little willingness' to the possibility that these new concepts we have received, could be real, could be true. The best example I can think of at this moment is a belief that many of us buy into, that a certain disease, 'runs in our families'. Yes, I know that the insurance companies have their actuarial tables and even book after book, written by doctors exist, that assure us, that if a certain illness was with your father, mother, grandparents or even great grandparents, it's a medical certainty, that you or someone in your family, will inherit, that particular illness.

Well I'm here to tell you, that Eighteen years with A Course In Miracles and Course Psychotherapy has changed my mind on this matter. I no longer believe or accept the idea that I inherited the worst traits, Mom or Dad, had to teach me. My father accepted his first ulcer at age 37 and my mother had her first heart attack at age 39. Now if they were foolish enough to accept these problems as their truth at that time, it is not in any way disrespectful or unloving of me, to not follow their example, by and preferring to . . . remain Healthy. Notice if you will, that Dad's ulcer followed Mom's heart attack. Is it not conceivable that Dad was so worried, seeing Mom in a hospital, for the first time, tubes connected to and coming out of Mom's body, what could be more frightening, or, painful, seeing someone you love, helplessly lying in a hospital bed, fearing that that person you love, might soon die.

Even now, I can recall my fears, standing at the side of Mom's hospital bed, having seen the look on Dad's face, which telegraphed

*A Course In Miracles and Psycotherapy, Purpose, Process and Practice published by the Foundation For Inner Peace, Glen Ellen, CA.

his doubt and fear. I'm sure all of us have gone through a period of time, where we have experienced a similar happening. The message here is do not accept the belief that anything runs in your family, or, that since Mom, Dad, Grandmother, Grandfather, Uncle Al, or Aunt Bertha had a specific illness, that it has to run in your family. This is the first step in reversing the mistaken belief that since someone on your family tree has had a problem, due to genetics, you must have the 'supposed illness' . . . remember it's only an illusion, as well.

My kid sister Norma had a problem accepting this concept and struggled with illness for most of her short adult life. In her thinking, she believed, that since Mom had her first heart attack at age 39, that she too could expect her heart attack at the same age. Guess what, she didn't disappoint herself and was in the hospital, just like her Mother, many years earlier. I watched in horror, year after year, as Norma put herself through this terrible ordeal, believing all the while that it was something, someone else, 'doing this to her'. I saw her buy into the family belief that diabetes ran in our family as well and try as I did, to explain what she was doing to herself . . . nothing seemed to get through and she left her body, many years earlier, than she needed to.

My baby sister, Mom and Dad have been wonderful teachers to me and as I write about them and all of the wonderful lessons they have provided for me, I am reminded, that we do not have to deceive ourselves any longer, believing that we are helpless, nor do we have to accept any untruths about the wonderful Healing abilities we all possess . . . through GOD.

Remember what so many of us have learned, through our studies of the Course . . .

'If you are not experiencing the Peace of GOD,
It is because, you have chosen, not to listen.'

*A Course in Miracles is published by the Foundation For Inner Peace, Glen Ellen, CA.

My Thoughts

Spirit Speaks

In 1978, I was given the marvelous booklet to print entitled The Song Of Prayer, on Prayer, Forgiveness, Healing. This was the last book I was to print, where Jesus and the Holy Spirit talked directly to and through Helen Schuckman (I thought).

When Helen left her body, I felt that the Holy Spirit and Jesus were finished with their communications, at least as far as I was concerned, but that is not the way it worked out. In 1988 I received a manuscript from a woman, I had never met, by the name of Jana Kelly, who lived in suburban Detroit, and in her cover letter, told me that she was a former school teacher. She also mentioned that she had been teaching yoga for some fifteen years and had begun to study the Course in September of 1985. Jana went on to say that she had continued her teaching/learning as A Course In Miracles study group facilitator at a Unity Church and was convinced that the Course, was her path. One day as she was reading a lesson in the text an overwhelming urge came over her to pick up a pencil to write a letter to a brother, who she knew was in pain. She resisted, because she felt that she had nothing wise to say to him, yet as she puts it, the urge to write the letter was so driving, that she gave up her resistance, gathered paper and pencil and began to write. Throughout that day, Jana says that she experienced many different emotions and she also says that she clearly heard the words from the Course:

'Step back and let Him lead the Way.'

Later, that same day Jana says that she clearly heard a message from what she believed to be the Voice for GOD, which she calls Spirit, requesting Jana to scribe for Him, to write Messages for herself and others. With that, Jana's journey as a scribe for the Holy Spirit, had begun. In April of 1988, I finished the first printing of Jana's Messages which she called Spirit Speaks and is subtitled Messages To A Student of 'A Course In Miracles' and this most extraordinary book contains more than one hundred messages, which I and most everyone else who reads this book, believe, truly is the voice of the Holy Spirit. I am reprinting my favorite, see if you don't find it helpful . . .

---

* *The Song of Prayer, published by the Foundation For Inner Peace, Glen Ellen, CA.*
* *Spirit Speaks, by Jana Kelly, published by Mind and Miracles, Ft. Lauderdale, FL.*

THE DANCE
November 9, 1987

'Maintain your peace through all. "How can this be done?" you ask. By remembering who you are. 'How can I maintain peace when others confront me, when others are in pain that affects me, when it seems that all around me there is fear and mistrust?' You can maintain your peace by remembering who your brothers are. Say, 'There is a Holy Son of GOD. There is a brother who loves me in his heart. There is a brother who is dancing the dance of life to the song he has selected.' When the songs are in harmony, your dance and his are one. You partner beautifully and feel the oneness. When your song and his are different, you cannot dance together for awhile. The melodies are discordant, the dance seems chaotic, the dancers stumble and falter for the flow is gone.

But remember again who you are. Remember that underneath all of earth's many melodies, is One Ancient Song so beautiful that it encompasses all the songs man ever wrote. When you all hear the song, the dance becomes Divine.

Be peaceful because even though each dancer in your life does not contribute to your dance, he is perfect in his own. Remember who your brother is. He is a Child of GOD on his way home. He is learning just as you are. He is being Healed at every moment. Do not analyze each experience or try to understand the discordant dance. You only understand your own.

'In the discord, I know not what to do or say!' Your doing or saying does not help or hurt any situation. Your doing or saying only helps you dance your dance more smoothly. Experience what you do or say as your lessons and incorporate them into your melody. How they affect your brother is the Holy Spirit's business, not yours. Holy Spirit will Heal. Your job is to offer love and acceptance and do your dance. Your part is to continue to see even through eyes of confusion or pain, that your brother is a Holy Son of GOD.

Say over and over . . .

'Bless you my brother. You and I are Holy Sons of GOD. We are going Home together Bless you, bless you, bless you!'

Maintain your peace. Herein is the way to harmonize the

melodies so that the many dances become the One.

When it seems impossible, know that ego is whispering in your ear. Turn your head away from him and listen to My Voice. I offer you love. I see you guiltless. I see you Healed. Peace to you, my child. You are dearly loved. Allow yourself to accept that gift. Receive it now.

In the last message from Spirit, in Jana's book, we are given some more wonderful Loving advice and it seems appropriate to share it with you. It's titled LEARNING ABOUT LOVE and it reads like this:

LEARNING ABOUT LOVE
January 25, 1988

'Human beings who don't love are in constant pain. Loving is the only emotion humans can experience, and when they deny this to themselves by withholding love from self or others, they are choosing misery.

In the Course, you're learning that GOD is Love, Creation is Love, the One is Love, Reality is Love, You are Love, and your brother is Love. That idea is so monumental that it makes you doubt your understanding about love, you become impotent, and therefore are unable to express or even receive love. Just as there is only One Creator and many Co-Creators within the One; there is only One Love, with many expressions of Love within the One. That is why it seems that there are different kinds of love in the world of form. All love shares the same Source and therefore, all love is the expression of that One Source. But you humans must learn this bit by bit, by experiencing love from many perspectives. Earth is the playground and schoolroom of love. In the world of form, your task is to learn about Love and Forgiveness. This is the only helpful learning available on this planet. That is why you're here. If you knew all about love, you wouldn't be in the world of form, you'd be in Heaven! No expression of love on earth is little. And no expression of love on earth is limited, if you use it to connect yourself to your Self!

Any thought which maintains or strengthens the idea that love is not real, is preserving the idea of 'hell.' To analyze love, chases it away. To reject love, delays your happiness. To withhold love from yourself or your brothers, causes the Son of GOD much pain. Rejecting any love experience or any opportunity to extend love, is a denial of your purpose on earth, and causes suffering. Forgiveness is just yourself inviting love's return after ego has denied it, or rejected it, or refused it entry.

So I say to you, shower yourself with love. Delight in all of its expressions. Accept every brother's attempts at expressing love, realizing that every attempt at loving is a holy lesson and pleases the Father. Be generous about love, love good books, love learning, love music, love animals, love nature, love your work, love your play, love good food, love excitement, love silence, love sharing, love ceremony, love GOD'S Word, love fun, love mystery, love beauty, love the known, love the unknown, love feeling good, love yourself, and love your Brother! Be simple about love. Be fearless about love. Be expressive through love. That is all. Peace to you, loved one.'

The balance of Spirit Speaks is filled with many more loving messages and presents to the reader, the student and to all of us a 'unique guidance' as to what our mission here on this planet, is all about. It not only gives us instruction and encouragement . . . but shares the message of 'living in the Light.'

Ask the Holy Spirit

If there is a Trinity, a threesome, a one two three, I would have to define the Trinity as GOD, the Holy Spirit and Jesus and all of us. Of that trio, the only man of the group, we're told, is Jesus. What was and still is startling to the world, is that we're told that Jesus is a Son of GOD the same as you and I. As a matter of fact in the Teacher's Manual, Book III, Page 83, we are told that 'The name of Jesus is the name of one who was a man but saw the face of Christ in all his brothers and remembered GOD. I had some problem, getting to believe that this could be true but ultimately, I came to accept and even believe that this much was true. The Holy Spirit was another matter, for me. The Course assures us that whenever we find ourselves in trouble, in doubt, in fear, not knowing which direction to go, or any decision we need to make, we are told we must ask the Holy Spirit, in order to go in the right direction, or to get the correct answer to the decision, we feel we need to make. After awhile of struggling with issues, decisions and even business, I finally learned to 'turn over' all of my problems, questions, and decisions, simply because I finally had the fullest confidence, in Holy Spirit's ability to do and get 'the job done'. As a result, a great many of the things that plagued me, years ago, no longer plague me today. As a matter of fact, even in business, where most of my telephone calls were of a complaining nature, I observed that turning 'the supposed problem' over to the Holy Spirit, always seemed to result in my being able to drop my fear, of whatever the problem or person presented. It was to me, like having a big brother taking care of your problems for you, no matter what those problems seemed to be.

Often, of late, people have approached me with questions of how to 'get over' various types of abuse, that they have dealt with, all of their life. First, I question if they have asked the Holy Spirit to assist. Some answer yes, but then add that H.S. didn't hear them, and that nothing has happened. I'm always reminded of the great line, 'GOD, give me patience, and I want it right now', when I hear someone complaining that Holy Spirit has not addressed their issues. Even after many people ask H.S. for the help, which we are guaranteed will come, many of us still seem to hold on to the pain of the experience. How can they be helped? Sometimes, we in the big dream, the illusion, become impatient and start to doubt, that our requests, our prayers, will go unanswered. Not everything happens as we would have it happen and further what we sometimes seem to forget is that if our wishes are not in the best interests of every single one involved, the Holy Spirit will find the way that is in the best interests of everyone involved. There's no favoring one . . . at the expense of another brother.

Remember also that the ego would try with everything ego has, to delay, have you resist, and try to prevent, the Healing. At times when you hear or feel ego's interference, just try to remember, that whatever it is that might be bugging you, is all an illusion, it never really happened, anyway.

If a crime was committed, it would be difficult for us to accept, that it was an illusion, that it never really happened, and yet that is precisely what we are asked to accept, if we are going to remain peaceful. The ego will try to convince you, that it is all real. The reality is, that no crime was committed. Try and see the accused person as your brother, as the Light, the very same Light, that you and I, truly are. If the crime seems to have been committed against you personally, then we must try to see the perpetrator as the person 'sent' to us to help us learn the lessons we have come to learn, the lessons of Love and Forgiveness.

The other day, a woman called me and said she was having great difficulty understanding the principles of the Course and she asked if there were any up and coming lectures or workshops going on in Florida, that might clarify for her, what this Course is trying to say. I told her that indeed we had some events involving clarification but as I talked to her, I sensed a great deal of pain and asked her where she lived, and since it was only about a thirty minute drive, I asked her if she would like to come over and just talk, one on one. She said she'd have to call me back in a few minutes, to let me know and I said, that would be fine. She called back about fifteen minutes later and about an hour and a half later, we were sitting in my living room and I was giving her my All Healing Is Through GOD, workshop. She was like a sponge drinking in everything I was explaining and after about three hours, or so, she said that so many things that she was experiencing difficulty with, were cleared up, but still there was a sense of unhappiness and even depression, that I was picking up on.

With tears running down her cheeks, she finally shared with me that she had been troubled with a 'problem' that had been with her, all of her life and could we take a few moments to possibly address her problem. I consented to listen and the 'problem' that she shared with me was certainly from the world's viewpoint, was a tough one, but aren't they all. She shared with me that she was the child of two people who never married and further, that, her mother and father conceived her on a first date, a one night stand. In her next thirty one years she never asked her mother, who or what her father was about and as she put it, she locked out any thoughts of what or who her father was. In her thinking she didn't wish to give him a thought or wonder whether or not, he existed. Her mother went along with this silence for all those years and it wasn't until she reached her thirty first birthday that she actually started to think, who is he, what is he?

She finally approached her mother and asked, was her father alive and if so, where was he? Her mother told her that he was indeed alive as far as she knew and gave this sad young woman her father's family name and wished her daughter, good luck in tracking her father down. She told me that she didn't have the courage to make the phone calls in the beginning and had a friend, do it for her. Amazingly, she tracked down the father and at first he denied the whole episode. After giving her dad information as to how, where, when etc, her father finally said OK it's possible and at the young woman's insistence, a meeting was arranged in Florida and the big day was actually going to come.

As she described it to me their first meeting was anything but loving and she was most uncomfortable and couldn't wait to get out of Florida and get back to her native state and more loving people and relationships. A short time later, still very depressed by the whole episode, she decided to give it another try and arranged to come back to Florida, to seek Healing. She had started her study of A Course In Miracles, found it tough going, and she was looking for someone who might be able to clarify, what the twelve hundred plus pages, were trying to say. She had been here in Florida and as she put it, ready to turn around and give it all up. She was sleeping at her father's factory and she felt unwanted, unloved and uninvited. It seemed to me that if she went back now, that this problem would not go away and that unless this were turned over to the Holy Spirit, right now, she would be unhappy for the rest of her life. I reminded her of what I had found out in my lifetime thus far . . . is . . . that on our own, we are totally unable to handle anything . . . but with the Holy Spirit's Help, we can handle everything. She understood and for the first time that day, I saw a smile. We continued to talk about what she should do and not do and she determined that for the first time in her thirty two years, she didn't have to handle her supposed problems, by herself. The load, her load, was suddenly lightened and she was peaceful with the knowledge that she had found something, someone, capable of lightening her load, everyone's load. All she, all we need to do is to ask the Holy Spirit.

She left my home that day with a renewed joy, a feeling of peace and the depression, that came in with her, was gone The whole Healing had taken four hours and both of us were, It's recipients. I am reminded here of three very important things.

1. *'There is no order of difficulty in miracles'*
2. *'The answer always is Love and Forgiveness'*
3. *'ASK THE HOLY SPIRIT'*.

Inner Peace is our birth right, reclaim it now.

---

* All quotes from A Course in Miracles, published by the Foundation For Inner Peace, Glen Ellen, CA.

"I Could See Peace Instead Of This"

In 1989, Spirit had me make the move from Long Island, New York, to Fort Lauderdale, Florida. The guidance was clear and my Inner Voice told me to remain still and not pursue any avenues of making a living, at this time. For me, a man used to keeping busy eighteen to twenty hours a day, this was a most unusual and difficult request. Nevertheless, knowing full well, that Spirit had plans for me . . . as usual, I listened. For a month, a full thirty one days, I just sat quietly, meditating and waiting. One day the mailman delivered a letter, which was originally mailed to our address in Farmingdale, New York and then forwarded to me in Florida. The letter had been mailed from Florida and bore the name and address on the corner of the envelope, of a man I did not know, and a town, I had not yet heard of. On opening the letter and reading it, the neatly typed words read pretty much as follows:

Dear Mr. Steinberg:

You don't know me, but I knew your cousin Paul. It was your cousin Paul Steinberg who actually turned me on to A Course In Miracles, some years ago. I had received a flyer announcing that Paul Steinberg would be talking in Louisiana and I flew my plane to investigate what this Course In Miracles, was about. I listened to his talk for two days and those two days, changed my life. I now have been with the Course for several years and have found it to be Truth, and the essence on how, to live one's life. The reason for this letter, is to let you know that Paul in his talks, spoke about you and I want to extend an invitation to you, that if you are ever in Florida, please call me and we will most definitely get together.

The letter was signed, *with love, Herb Harrington.*

As I read that letter, the Guidance was to pick up the phone and call and introduce myself to Herb Harrington and I did. The voice on the other end of the line greeted me in a cheerful manner. I introduced myself and told Herb that I had received his letter and that there was no need to wait for my arrival in Florida, as I was already living in Florida. He seemed to be delighted, to be meeting me, even

---

* Workbook Lesson #34, A Course in Miracles, published by the Foundation For Inner Peace, Glen Ellen, CA.

if it was over the telephone and we spoke about Paul, the Course and many other things. Herb asked if there was any possibility of my coming up to the Orlando area in the near future and since Judy and I were waiting for our Guidance and had nothing planned, we agreed to visit Herb and his wife Jane, the following week.

A week later, Judy and I found ourselves driving North on the Florida Turnpike, and about four hours later found ourselves in a small suburb of Orlando, called Castleberry, at the lovely home of Herb and Jane Harrington. Jane had prepared a lite lunch and we all sat outside on their patio, looking out over a very peaceful lake and I remember thinking, this was the way to live. The three days we spent in the Orlando area were spent in meeting many of the people, living in that area, who were involved with the Course and I remember Herb driving us to the Unity Church in downtown Orlando and there was a group of people, sitting in a circle and I told my story of the printing of A Course In Miracles. We had brought some of our books and tapes with us and I was amazed that a great deal of our materials were being purchased. The following evening Herb took us to another group of brothers and sisters and again most everyone was supportive and I started to realize that Spirit was showing me what it was I was to do in Florida. The last night that Judy and I were to spend in Orlando, Herb introduced us to a close friend of his, by the name of Bo Abernethy and what I did not know at that time was that Bo was one of the people that had started more study groups of the Course, than any one else in Florida. By the time Judy and I left the Orlando area . . . Spirit had shown me a new way of earning a living in my newly adopted state of Florida and a way to meet many, many new brothers and sisters, of a like Mind.

A few weeks after our Orlando trip, I started to plan, with Spirit's help, a series of three lecture/workshops, to be held in three cities in Florida, consisting of two days, Saturday and Sunday and that these weekends should focus on one of the major themes of the Course. My Guidance was to focus the lectures on the most important theme in the Course . . . Forgiveness and the cities selected were Fort Lauderdale, Orlando and Clearwater. I invited Herb and Bo to join me in doing the three weekends and we were on our way.

The first lecture was held in Fort Lauderdale and I lined up a lovely spacious room at a Marriott Hotel, just off of I-95, put together a brochure announcing the workshops, went to an old mailing list I had compiled years before and stuffed envelopes, licked stamps and actually got my mailing out.

Fort Lauderdale

The morning of our first Forgiveness workshop was a beautiful Saturday morning and as I left my condo in Bonaventure, I was to say the least, feeling real peaceful and expecting to have a wonderful weekend, with a large turnout of brothers and sisters. As I got on the newly completed interstate 595 driving east towards I-95, my mind started to wander a bit with thoughts about how everything had worked out with my move to Florida and how in listening to the Guidance of Spirit, my life seemed to really be working again. Before I knew what happened, I swung from the extreme right hand lane of the interstate, to the extreme left hand lane. As I looked to my right, I saw a young man, wearing a red tee shirt, with a red bandanna wrapped around his neck, looking at me and cursing. As I looked closer, I noticed that he was not wearing a red bandanna around his neck . . . it was his blood which apparently had travelled from his heart up to his neck and he was to say the least, very angry. Sensing that he needed a little or perhaps a lot of love, at that moment, I rolled down my window, slowed down so that we were driving abreast of each other, looked at him and hollered . . . forgive me, I didn't mean to cut you off. The invisible or should I say visible bandanna was still around his neck and with the angriest of stares, he yelled out at me . . . 'hey dickhead', did you buy your license in New York? I didn't realize until he screamed at me, that I still had my New York plates on the back of my car and I guess this infuriated him even more. Did I mention that he was driving a red pickup truck? Once again I figured I would try to apologize to my new found friend and as I looked in his direction once again, he took that moment to send me a gesture, I recognized from the Bronx and I assumed that he was not accepting any apology or was he ready to forgive me, for my cutting him off. I thought I should take one more stab at apologizing to him . . . after all, I was on my way to a Forgiveness workshop and this time I pulled out all the stops and once again

I pulled up along side of him and this time I spoke the words I knew, could not fail. I said as loud as I could and with as much feeling and sincerity as I could muster, and said, 'I love you' and with that said, I put my open hand up to my mouth and sent him a great big Dinah Shore kiss. This only seemed to infuriate him more and as I turned off on I-95 north and he continued straight on I-595 east . . . I remember thinking to myself . . . well I gave it my best shot. I then turned it over to the Holy Spirit and asked Spirit to help that young man to find his own inner peace as I had found mine. Now the lesson in this story as I see it, is that as long as you can take what appears to be an uncomfortable situation, or leave the scene dealing with attack of any description, feeling peaceful, feeling that you have offered Forgiveness to your brother and most importantly, your feeling totally peaceful . . . you have healed whatever the attack lesson, was all about.

You see the Healing, any Healing is one that leaves you totally peaceful. If the other person chooses to be miserable, chooses to be angry, chooses to be sick, over the seeming conflict, he or she cannot receive the healing, due to, their unforgiveness attitude. The message is clear, concise and true . . . Forgiveness is the most Healing emotion we possess.

Orlando

The following Saturday and Sunday was our Orlando workshop and after the success of Fort Lauderdale, I figured that Spirit had some other 'goodies' in store for us in Orlando. . . and I was right. For Orlando, I had rented a room in a Holiday Inn and when I saw our Orlando group assembled, I had the room set up in a circle as opposed to the traditional theater style. As was our usual procedure, we opened with a meditation and our second Forgiveness weekend was on it's way. I remember real well some of that weekend's activities but I guess the one that stands out most in my memory is the final session on the Saturday of that weekend. As I mentioned, we were all in a circle, sitting opposite each other. On one side there was a couple who were both suffering with cancer and directly opposite them was another couple who had lost their daughter in a tragic automobile accident. The focus on that particular session was that through the Forgiveness process, and only through the Forgiveness process, could both couples and everyone else suffering with any type of problem, could peace be achieved . . . peace in thinking . . . which ultimately would translate into Healing.

A heated argument was breaking out between the four people, the two with cancer and the couple involved with the death of their daughter in the tragic accident. The whole room was becoming a battlefield and everyone present including me was suddenly involved in an attack session and the pressure was rising. Bo Abernethy who was leading that particular segment, was the only totally calm person in the room and very serenely, without saying a word, suddenly and slowly raised his right hand as though he was going to take an oath and very softly said: 'I could see peace instead of this'. He repeated again, even more softly this time: 'I could see Peace instead of this'. Of course this is Workbook Lesson number 34 from Book II, Page 51, from the Course and suddenly the room became totally still. The entire room was suddenly quiet and peaceful. This was indeed one of the most effective demonstrations, I had ever seen, in all of the years, I had been with the Course. The room and everyone in it had gone from being on and in, a battlefield, to a holy place where a feeling of peace prevailed. That Saturday afternoon ended soon after and I and everyone else in the room that afternoon, knew that something unique and different had happened.

The next morning, all of us reassembled at the appointed time and after the opening meditation, the man who had told us that he had the cancer, asked if he might address the group, before we started our session. I was the moderator for this particular segment, and of course I told him he could speak. He started to tell us, that for the past eight months, since his diagnosis of terminal cancer, he had been going several times a month for chemo-therapy and had been given some sort of pain killers, by his doctor. He shared with the group, that each and every night at the same time, he would awaken from his sleep and with the severe pain he was feeling, he needed to reach over to his bottle of pain killers, take a couple of capsules and wait for the pain to subside, before he could go back to sleep. He shared with us that last night (Saturday) once again he awoke with this terrible pain that he had experienced every night for the past

---

Lesson 34, Book II, Workbook of A Course in Miracles is published by the Foundation For Inner Peace, Glen Ellen, CA.

eight months and instinctively, he reached out for his bottle of pain killers. As his left hand wrapped around the bottle, he said and I quote, what he saw, 'was the vision of Bo Abernethy suddenly appearing before him and he said he clearly heard and saw Bo, right hand raised up, repeating the title of Lesson 34 . **'I could see peace instead of this.'** As though there was a prearranged signal, as he recognized and accepted this vision, his pain started to retreat in a downward direction and most amazingly, his pain completely disappeared. As he continued with this amazing story, he said that for the first time in eight months, he was able to go back to sleep, without calling upon his pain killers, and he pledged that he would try to remember to repeat that very same procedure, every night from then on. Now, was this a miracle? You better believe it was. The Course tells us that a miracle is a change in our perception, a change of mind . . . to Mind. Did this man experience the Atonement, certainly. His miracle took him from his place of ego thinking to the place of the true Self.

I and everyone else in the room had been present to see and hear that a brother asked for and received the miracle and then was the recipient of the Atonement (the result of the miracle). One more lesson for me, one more lesson for the man with the cancer, one more lesson for every person in that room. That beautiful weekend on Forgiveness, that beautiful Saturday and Sunday, in Orlando.

Clearwater

The last Forgiveness workshop was to take place in one of Florida's most beautiful cities, the city of Clearwater. Once again we rented a lovely room in a Holiday Inn and a new group of people were present. There was a couple who had asked if they could drive up with me to attend this workshop as they were both experiencing a great deal of physical pain and they were anxious to see if this 'stuff' really worked.

The ride from Fort Lauderdale to Clearwater was filled with questions not only about Forgiveness and how it worked but also how we could possibly create and buy into illness and was Healing of their illness's really possible? The man's problem was, that a

---

* Workbook Lesson #34, A Course in Miracles, published by the Foundation For Inner Peace, Glen Ellen, CA.

chronic back condition had gotten so severe, that he was living out his life, almost as a cripple. It was almost impossible for him to sit, to stand, to bend to bathe, or even wipe his own behind. His wife's problem was a deep fear of many issues, but mostly a deep fear of her husband, which was leading her to a most severe case of depression and if continued, a much too early death. Everything in their relationship was to say the least, volatile. Their relationship was hostile, fearful, filled with anxieties and extremely explosive. On the ride up to Clearwater, I raised my hand many, many times and repeated Lesson 34, repeating **'I could see peace instead of this'**, **'I could see peace instead of this.'**

By the time we got to the Holiday Inn, not only were these two civil towards each other, they were actually loving. Saturday in Clearwater went real well and that Saturday night, this man with the bad back, invited many of the people at the workshop to dinner and I heard him telling a young doctor who was present at our workshop, that the reason she was experiencing the terrible stomach pains she had complained of, during that day, were all due to the great stress, that she had created in her life and that the only way she could rid herself of her pain was to forgive her father, whom she had perceived, had created her pain. The miracle was happening, I could hear it, I could feel it, I could sense it. Soon . . . I was certain, I would see the Atonement. I didn't have to wait very long. This man who needed to carry a special chair with him, wherever he went, this man who couldn't sit, couldn't stand, couldn't bend, couldn't wipe his own behind, by the Sunday of that very same weekend of our Forgiveness workshop in Clearwater, Florida, was actually out of pain. He was able to bend over without experiencing any back pain at all, and was able to do things, using his back, that he had not been able to do, in years. His attitude towards his wife that next day was concern, caring and most definitely loving. She was full of smiles, beaming from the love he was sending, and the sadness, the gloom, the depression and the unhappiness, were gone.

As we drove back to Fort Lauderdale that Sunday night, I was filled with the most beautiful feeling from the many Healings, I had witnessed in Clearwater, that weekend. The three Forgiveness weekends we had experienced in Fort Lauderdale, Orlando and Clearwater, clearly had been arranged by the Holy Spirit to show

---

* Workbook Lesson #34, A Course in Miracles, published by the Foundation For Inner Peace, Glen Ellen, CA.

each and everyone of us in attendance, that there is no need to be unhappy, there is no need to be ill, there is no need to be fearful, and that you too . . .

COULD SEE PEACE INSTEAD OF THIS.

Attitudinal Healing

When Dr. Gerald Jampolsky started the first Attitudinal Healing Center in Tiburon, California, I doubt that he had any idea that the concept he originated, would become a way of life, for so many people. Dr. Jampolsky's original approach to Attitudinal Healing was primarily working with terminally ill children. This happened when he needed a 'change of perception' because his own life, as he puts it, was not working. Making the shift, he found himself working in an oncology ward of a hospital and suddenly he became aware that children facing cancer, were struggling emotionally and spiritually as well as physically. He realized that children had no one place that he knew of, where they could go to discuss their concerns or fears, about 'dying'. He soon had a peer group started, where children who felt fearful, isolated and most angry about their disease, could begin to experience, perhaps for the first time, peace and love, by reaching out and supporting, other children. This approach was so successful, that other groups for children and their parents, were soon started. As mentioned previously in this book, Attitudinal Healing Centers have sprung up all over this country and all over the world. The best definition of Attitudinal Healing that I know of, is the definition that appears in Genevieve Weirich's book, Attitudinal Healing A Guide For Groups and Individuals, which she published in 1988. It goes like this:

Definition Of Attitudinal Healing

'Attitudinal Healing' is the process of releasing our fears so that we can experience our natural state which is to be loving and peaceful. As we choose to change our fearful attitudes, we are free to let go of the past and to live in the moment, to forgive ourselves and others, to feel our connectedness with others, and to feel loved. The healed mind trusts that the world is governed by a power in it but not of it; that power is love, the most important healing power in the world. And that power will guide us to the extent we trust it and remember to call upon it.'

Attitudinal Healing is 'health and healthy living, inner peace

---

* *Attitudinal Healing, A Guide For Groups and Individuals*, by Genevieve Weirich, published by Cambridge Publishing, Inc., available through Mind and Miracles, Ft. Lauderdale, FL.

and the healing process and letting go of painful, fearful attitudes. When we let go of fear, only Love remains and that Love is, letting go of fear. Love is the only healing force in the world and our natural state of being.'

12 Principles of Attitudinal Healing

1. The essence of our being is Love.
2. Health is inner peace Healing is letting go of fear.
3. Giving and receiving are the same.
4. We can let go of the past and of the future.
5. Now is the only time there is and each instant is for giving.
6. We can learn to love ourselves and others by forgiving rather than judging.
7. We can become love finders rather than fault finders.
8. We can choose and direct ourselves to be peaceful inside regardless of what is happening outside.
9. We are students and teachers to each other.
10. We can focus on the whole of life rather than the fragments.
11. Since Love is eternal, death need not be viewed as fearful.
12. We can always perceive ourselves and others as either extending love or giving a call for help.

Listed above are what we can call the essential concepts or principals of Attitudinal Healing. Like the Ten Commandments, what these 12 principles really represent are a guide to what I believe the Holy Spirit would have us do, observe and practice in order to get back to our 'natural state', which is to be totally peaceful. Let's discuss them one by one, as I do in my lectures and I'll give you my thoughts on how they apply to me and perhaps to you.

1. The essence of our being is Love.

I often switch the words Love and GOD. At this point to me, they are one and the same. GOD is Love and Love is GOD. So to me the essence of our being is GOD. In the Course, we are told that

* A Course in Miracles, published by the Foundation For Inner Peace, Glen Ellen, CA.

each and everyone of us, without exception, are beautiful children of a Loving Father, in whom He is well pleased. We spend a good deal of our lives believing that GOD is angry with us. What I've learned from my studies and publishing efforts is that GOD is never angry with us, no matter what terrible thing we perceive, that we have done. GOD never punishes us, simply because GOD never condemns us, any of us. GOD sees each and every one of us His Children as 'Perfection, Perfect Creations,' again no exceptions. What we need to remember is, that we did not create ourselves, we are the Creations of a Loving GOD. If we can remember our Essence, we can have Healing.

2. Health is inner peace. Healing is letting go of fear.

In the introduction of A Course In Miracles we are told, 'The opposite of Love is fear, but what is all encompassing can have no opposite.' All of the negative emotions encompassed under the word fear are all truly one and the same. Most people opening the Course for the first time are surprised to see the words 'the opposite of love is fear,' because we have always believed that the opposite of love is hate. If one examines what hate is all about does it not really boil down to just being another form of fear.

A central point in the Course is that 'health is inner peace' which is stating for me, that if we are not peaceful, we are in a state of un peace or chaos. Therefore if we find ourselves not enjoying peace, the chances become greater for us to be sick and we must take a closer look at what we are thinking and what we are doing, which is diverting us away from being peaceful. Love is our natural inheritance and since everything we see and think is a matter of our own perception, what we conclude and how we handle what we conclude is surely responsible, for how we act. We cannot blame anyone outside of ourselves, for the 'supposed' problem and it answers the question that if two people are experiencing the same problem and one seems to be able to handle the problem, what constitutes the difference. The answer is, only their perception or the way they choose to see and handle the ` supposed' problem. Yes, one person can still be peaceful, regardless of the 'supposed' problem and the other person experiencing the very same problem, might drive themselves towards self destruction. It is clearly the perception

*A Course in Miracles is published by the Foundation For Inner Peace, Glen Ellen, CA.

that we choose and only changing our attitude, will make the difference.

3. Giving and receiving are the same.

When I started studying the Course in the late 1970's, I believed that if you gave something away, it was gone. If someone had told me that when you give away something that you get back or receive a greater reward or that giving and receiving are one and the same, I would have laughed in their faces. My belief was that once something leaves your hands, it was gone. The thing that changed my mind real quick was when I got involved with the Course and started giving out 'unconditional love,' I immediately started to receive greater amounts of 'unconditional love,' then I was giving out. What I found was that people were much more loving, not for what they could get, but more loving because they were receiving love in greater abundance. I also had this principle clarified for me when I observed that a great many wealthy people gave heavily to charity and other philanthropies and the more they gave, the greater amounts they seemed to receive back. Further it was their resolve to continue doing so because they completely understood this principle. I think it is safe to state that abundance is totally a state of mind and has nothing to do with how much, or how little you have in the bank account. Physical abundance without Spiritual Abundance is impossible.

4. We can let go of the past and of the future.

This principle is very important in the Course. It deals with 'letting go' of the past. We are reminded that what has already happened cannot be undone, even though it is an illusion. How many of us spend time dwelling in the past, reliving and reliving events and circumstances of the past. Yet there is nothing we can do about undoing anything that has occurred in the past. And what about the future? Who really knows or can predict what is in anyone's future. Even the very best Psychics are wrong at times and yet many of us hold ourselves back from wonderful things because someone predicts an uncertain or negative result.

The principle from the Course that best addresses this principle is to live, totally and completely in the NOW. Being happy, and

---

*A Course in Miracles, published by the Foundation For Inner Peace, Glen Ellen, CA.

peaceful in the NOW is really all there is and should be. If you feel the need to keep dredging up something that occurred some years ago, or even twenty minutes ago, just determine to let it go. You can change those thoughts of yesterday or tomorrow into thoughts of only NOW. The Course tells us that thoughts of the past, even if they start out as happy thoughts, usually very quickly turn into negative thoughts. In short, let go of the past . . . let go of the future and make NOW the very best time for yourself.

5. Now is the only time there is and each instant is for giving.

Notice the last two words in this principle is for giving. Those are two very interesting words and I have the tendency to make the two words into one word, that word being forgiving. The bottom line and the focus of A Course In Miracles is about Forgiving and Forgiveness. We are told that Healing cannot take place until there is Forgiveness and that the only way we can achieve peace for ourselves, is thru Forgiveness. Certainly this begins with ourselves and the time for us for giving ourselves the greatest gift, we can give ourselves is NOW, the only time there is . . . the greatest gift, being Forgiveness, which is guaranteed to lead us to peace and happiness.

6. We can learn to love ourselves and others by forgiving rather than judging.

The Course spends a great deal of time, reminding us that we are totally incapable of judging. It tells us that the only capable Judge is the Holy Spirit, due to the fact, that only the Holy Spirit is aware of past, present and future. If we could focus on recognizing 'our true Identity', it would be impossible for us to feel guilt or fear. When we try to judge, we are always incorrect in our judgments, due to the fact, that we are judging thru our ego minds. I'm reminded of the old Indian proverb, *'unless you've walked a mile in my moccasins, how can you know anything about me'*. Surely we are totally incapable of assessing motive in any case, yet if we apply forgiveness each and every time, we are assured the ability to completely relieve all pain, all distress and all discomfort.

7. We can become love finders rather than fault finders.

This is important because many of us have a tendency to meet

---

* A Course in Miracles, published by the Foundation For Inner Peace, Glen Ellen, CA.

someone and make a 'snap' judgment about that person. That judgment is usually quite the reverse, of what the truth usually is. Though people or situations may look a certain way outwardly, it is usually not a true indicator of what that person or situation truly is, as a fact. The Course advises that every encounter is a Holy Encounter and is never the result of an accident. That person or situation has entered our life, for a reason, for a purpose. Perhaps to help us learn a specific lesson, that we came into these bodies, to learn. For example, we might be walking down a street and encounter someone and at that moment, for some reason, feel fear. We then build this whole scenario of fear thoughts, around that person. We may cross the street to distance ourselves from that person and may even lose our peace for a time afterward, just wondering 'what was that person, up to?' We somehow build a whole illusion in our thinking. The Course teaches us to see the Christ in every single one of our brothers and sisters. By finding and seeing the Light in everyone, instead of trying to find the faults in GOD'S other children, we are guaranteed, that they will see the Light in us. 'There are no neutral thoughts' so the mission becomes, send out Love and be a Love finder.

8. We can choose and direct ourselves to be peaceful inside regardless of what is happening outside.

Returning to the Workbook lesson 34 mentioned earlier 'I could see peace instead of this', most certainly points out that it is our choice, whether we make the decision to see a matter peacefully or not. It reminds me of a trip I made some years ago to address a group of Course brothers and sisters, that also were involved in 12 step programs. When I exited the plane and hailed a cab, the driver quickly engaged me in conversation and one of the things he was quick to point out was, had I any idea, that Detroit was suffering with an eighteen percent unemployment problem. I remember thinking about his question for a moment and answered, that no, I was not aware of Detroit's eighteen percent unemployment problem, but countered back much more cheerfully, had he ever thought about, if what he said was true, happily Detroit, had a full eighty two percent employment. He admitted, that he had not thought of it that way. It is like the 'glass half empty or half full perception lesson. It truly is

* A Course in Miracles, published by the Foundation For Inner Peace, Glen Ellen, CA.

'what and how', we choose to see and feel, that determines our reality and how we feel.

So regardless of what seems to be happening outside of ourselves, we can choose to be peaceful and see any circumstance in the most positive light. The Course also stresses the importance of asking Spirit's assistance in seeing things differently with Workbook lesson 28, Page 43 where He give us 'Above all else I want to see things differently.' Ask Spirit's help in changing from the ego way of seeing, to the Spirit way of knowing.

9. We are students and teachers to each other.

Some years ago I worked with a gentleman, a therapist, who told me that the most important lesson he had learned up to that time, was learned from his dog. He shared with me that one day, after a particularly stress filled day, he returned home, hoping for a nice quiet evening in which he could just be 'left alone.' As he sat down in his easy chair to relax, his dog, sensing my friend's need of love, put his two front paws up on my friend's easy chair and with love and affection, started licking my friend's face. As mentioned, my friend just wanted to be left alone and in his anger, the man kicked the dog in the ribs and the dog yelped, jumped up straight in the air, and immediately wheeled around and headed for the door. As the dog got to the door, he stopped and sensing his master's need for love, wheeled around, returned to the chair, this time the other side, again put his front paws up on the chair and proceeded to kiss his master's other cheek.

My friend, the therapist, told me he had learned the most important lesson of his life that day and had learned this most valuable lesson, from his dog. The lesson was 'Unconditional Love', a lesson that each and everyone of us, is here to learn. At the end of the Course, we learn that the illusion, the big dream is over when each and everyone of us, without exception, can see the Light in each and every one of our brothers and sisters, also without exception, that it is then and only then that we truly practicing 'Unconditional Love'.

10. We can focus on the whole of life rather than the fragments.

Recently there was a book that made it to the best sellers list,

---

A Course in Miracles, published by the Foundation For Inner Peace, Glen Ellen, CA.

which addressed and told us how, we could commit suicide. I have asked myself why anyone would wish to end their life (even if it is an illusion) when so many of us are fighting constantly, to stay in this dream. The obvious answer seems to be, that at that particular time, they are unable to find any joy in their lives. Whereas most of us can view a sunset, a child at play and feel love, others simply do not. They are unwilling to see the whole plan and are only focusing on what is going on with themselves or others, at that particular time. They are preferring to see just a small fragment of the situation, rather than seeing the whole picture, which of course is, that things will get better. It's like sitting in a plane, waiting to take off and the rain is coming down in buckets and you wonder what are you doing on this contraption and with the blackness surrounding you, your feeling is that no good can come from this experience, all because of this dark moment. Suddenly the plane is given permission from the tower to take off, you're airborne and after a few moments you are above the clouds . . . and all is well, once again. We all seem to have this tendency to be frightened by some event and I suspect that at that particular moment, we are focusing on a small fragment of life as opposed to the whole. When you find yourself in a frightening experience, any frightening experience, just remember that this is a learning experience and the experience is always teaching us to 'let go of the fear and remember our true Identity'.

11. Since love is eternal, death need not be viewed as fearful.

One of the things I have learned from the Holy Spirit and Jesus, is that we do not die. It has become very clear to me that a part of the message that Jesus has given us is, that there is no death. He came to teach us about Love and Forgiveness, but not about what seems to be a belief of ours, that we die. In the Course he shares with us that our bodies die but since we are not our bodies, we don't die. The 'real' us is Spirit, Soul but definitely not our body. We go on and on until this teaching/learning experience is no longer necessary and then we return to our Father's House (which in Truth, we never really left). It is not too difficult for me to accept this concept, since I have observed that in 1975 when I started to print this material called A Course In Miracles, there were less than three hundred people who thought this way and now there are millions of my

---

*A Course in Miracles is published by the Foundation For Inner Peace, Glen Ellen, CA.

brothers and sisters who accept this material as Truth. The language, and the words are heard on TV shows, radio, newspapers and in books and are coming out in rapid succession everywhere. One of the major reasons I feel that this is occurring, is due to our learning that we and our loved ones don't die and some of us are losing our fear of death. I find it far more comforting to think of any of the people in my special love relationship as still alive, as compared to being in a box, buried in the ground. Jesus has beautifully taught this lesson and I ask is there anyone who seriously could believe that a Teacher of GOD, with Jesus's knowledge, could have not jumped off the cross any time he chose to. Even at the urging of his friends to defend himself, he demonstrated no fear and no willingness to change what everyone at that time saw as certain death. One of the major things Jesus came to teach us was and is, that there is no death. His message clearly is not about the crucifixion, it is most certainly about the Resurrection, that he and we, do not die. When I was a kid, I heard and remember President Franklyn D. Roosevelt make a statement which said 'We have nothing to fear but fear itself'. I think I have come up with a better thought, which is, 'We have nothing to fear, not even fear.' That most certainly includes the fear of death.

12. We can always perceive ourselves and others as either extending love or giving a call for help.

A Course In Miracles tells us that all illness is a cry for love. People can and do perceive that they are not being loved, even when in fact, they have the love of the most important party, the love of GOD. This love of GOD is never, never taken away or in any way or action, withheld. GOD never stops loving any of His Children, which is again every single one of us. The Course makes this point crystal clear. Everyone of us has this unstoppable flow of GOD's Love and we have to know it, believe it and accept it as our truth. These principles work, because of our belief in their ability, to work. There is simply no illness, that we can invent, which GOD cannot help us to Heal.

These principles of Attitudinal Healing, I think outline for all of us that we can straighten out our thinking the moment we are willing to show a little willingness, to do so. I would like to share

---

*A Course in Miracles, published by the Foundation For Inner Peace, Glen Ellen, CA.

with you this very beautiful passage from the Text, Book I of the Course.

> *"Once you accept His plan*
> *as the one function that you would fulfill,*
> *there will be nothing else*
> *the Holy Spirit will not arrange for you*
> *without your effort.*
> *He will go before you*
> *making straight your path,*
> *and leaving no stones*
> *to trip on, and no obstacles*
> *to bar your way.*
> *Nothing you need will be denied you.*
> *Not one seeming difficulty*
> *but will melt away before you reach it.*
> *You need take thought for nothing,*
> *careless of everything*
> *except the only purpose*
> *that you would fulfill. "*

If you have not figured out as yet what that function the second line of the above is referring to . . . it is your function to be and remain Peaceful . . . given to us by GOD.

---

*A Course in Miracles, published by the Foundation For Inner Peace, Glen Ellen, CA.

Change your mind . . . To Change Your Life

I have learned by way of the Course, that following the dictates of the ego mind, we can accomplish nothing, zero, zip. So many of us spend our lives listening to ego, trying to prove to us that we are not what or whom we truly are . . . that is, *a beautiful Child of GOD . . . in Whom He is well pleased.* The ego would have us believe that we are the bodies we see, when we look into our mirrors. The Course reminds us that we are not our bodies but are in fact . . . Spirit. Along with our belief in ego, there is also a belief in pain, suffering, illness and death. These are all related to and about the body and even the big dream, the illusion seems very real and very frightening. Letting go of the fear of all of the above and getting started to accepting the Truth . . . the Way . . . and the Life, that is of GOD is not simple but it is easy. It is not quick but can happen in an instant . . . A Holy Instant. What you need to do is:

Change your mind . . . to change your life.

Jesus and the Holy Spirit have given us all, a wonderful means of doing this with the 365 Workbook lessons that comprise Book II of A Course In Miracles. Seemingly one for each and every day of the year, any year.

Somehow in a Spiritual/Psychological study as this is, it seems to take the individual Child of GOD and starts to introduce him or her to a way of seeing things differently. A way of reversing his or her thinking, a way to change their minds, so they can begin to change their lives.

The belief and acceptance of illness is precisely the reason illness exists at all. It starts as a thought, delivered by our ego mind, which seems to know it's job, which is delivering all of the bad news to us, whether we ask for it, or not. When the news is delivered thru mind to us that we can be sick, or to put it another way, when the first symptoms appear, it is only the acceptance that we either give or don't give, that accounts for us having the illness or dis-ease, or not having it. The acceptance of ego's thoughts that we can actually be ill, is what accounts for all illness, as I see it. Notice I said all, illness and dis-ease, because there is no way any illness exists, unless we give it birth and life. I know this sounds rather radical but that's

* A Course in Miracles, published by the Foundation For Inner Peace, Glen Ellen, CA.

the way I see it . . . in the NOW.

The thing that I have been able to do, which keeps me out of a doctor's office and has done that since 1975 is to not accept the belief that a beautiful child of GOD (me), in whom He is well pleased, truly can be or get . . . sick. At the first sign or symptom of anything, whether it is that familiar tickle that seems to come right before the cold, or the soreness developing in the throat, or any feeling, signaling that some form of upset or illness or dis-ease, is soon to arrive, this is the time to act. This moment when you feel the symptom, is the moment, to recognize that the ego is once again trying to prove to you that you are your body and not the *'beautiful child of GOD', in whom GOD is well pleased.*

At the moment you feel that first tickle, that first symptom, stop, get quiet, and ask the Holy Spirit for the help you need to see this situation differently. It is not at all important to even know what the problem you are perceiving is but it is all important in order to nip this negative thinking, which is creating the 'seeming' problem, to immediately ask for Holy Spirit's Help. This and this only, will work and deliver to you the Peace and Healing, that you seek.

As mentioned before . . . ego and the Holy Spirit, are on the job twenty four hours a day, every day. Absolutely no request is too trivial or unimportant for the Holy Spirit, to help you with.

It starts with *'changing your mind'.*

Material Things Do Not Deliver Peace Or Love

One of the material things I craved as a young business man was a Lincoln Mark IV automobile. Somehow, I thought that driving that sleek automobile with the spare tire look built into the trunk was a sign to the world, that the person driving this marvelous car . . . had made it. As things started to happen with me in business, in 1975, I leased a beautiful Lincoln Mark IV, dark brown, with a light tan leather roof and that car received a loving, babying treatment and love that no car had ever received before. Every night after wiping the days accumulation of dust off of the car, I would carefully deposit the car in my garage, being super careful that when I opened the door to get out, that no part of the door made contact with the concrete wall, to insure no scratches or nicks would mar the finish of this gorgeous car. After all, this was at that time, the material thing, that gave me status, indeed proved to the world, to my family and myself as well and showed, who I truly was . . . I thought.

Several years later, after we had already started our miracles group and were deep in study and doing Workbook lessons daily, one of the lessons that gave me (and most everyone in our group) the most difficulty was Lesson 1, in the Workbook. The lesson starts out with *'Nothing I see in this room (on this street, from this window, in this place) means anything'* and then goes on to say that *'This table does not mean anything.'* *'This chair does not mean anything'* and then very gently gets into the body parts and a little further down actually says *'That body does not mean anything'* and I wondered to myself, what the hell is this trying to tell us. I really did not at all, comprehend what this lesson was all about, but I was later to have an experience, that would once and forever teach me the true meaning of Lesson 1 of the Workbook.

As I was driving to my office on Long Island one day in my beautiful shiny Mark IV, the traffic light on Long Island Avenue changed from green to red, just as I approached it. Since, I've never been one to speed, I had plenty of time and room to come to a full stop and started to think about how wonderfully well things were going. My thoughts were focused on how sweet life had become, when suddenly I and my beautiful Mark IV was hit, hard, from

---

* Workbook, Book III of A Course in Miracles is published by the Foundation For Inner Peace, Glen Ellen, CA.

behind, by another vehicle. I was thrown forward and immediately snapped back and only the soft leather of the seat and the head rest stopped my flight. In that split second, while my body was being thrown forward and then backwards . . . I knew that the back of my car, the beautiful spare tire look, the tail lights, the trunk, my dream, my prized possession, had been totally demolished. As I opened the door of my now demolished automobile, I was ready to kill. I actually was experiencing and feeling savage rage and the need to attack this person that took my dream and destroyed it. In that split second as I opened my door I knew, that I would yank the creep who demolished my dream, out of his car and beat the living life out of him.

As I turned to my rear and started to walk towards my attacker's car . . . Lesson 1 of the Workbook popped into my mind.

> *'This table does not mean anything.'*
> *'This chair does not mean anything.'*
> *'This hand does not mean anything.'*
> and then . . .
> 'This car does not mean anything.'

Suddenly, in the short time and space of walking from my car to his, Lesson 1 made all the sense in the world. Would I, should I, lose my Inner Peace due to a hunk of metal, a material thing. The time to get from my car to his, was less than 30 seconds but in that 30 seconds, I completely understood what Lesson 1 was all about.

When I reached the door of the car that had crashed into me, my thoughts immediately turned to, was my brother injured, dead or what? As I opened the door to his car and pulled him out, I heard myself asking my brother if he was OK? I pulled him out of the car, placed him on the grass and when he came to, again I asked if he was OK? He looked up at me in a kind of daze, not realizing where he was or what had happened and in his dazed state of confusion looked at the back of my Mark IV and started to apologize and I'll never forget the look of fear on his face. At that moment all I saw was a brother in great pain and only Spirit knows what thoughts were going through this young man's mind. I asked him if he would like me to take him to a hospital and he declined. I asked him if he could move all the parts of his body, he tried and said he seemed to be OK and helped him to get up.

---

* Workbook, Book II of A Course in Miracles, published by the Foundation For Inner Peace, Glen Ellen, CA.

His car, the front end was also somewhat demolished but amazingly the engine was still running and driveable and I remember helping him back into his car. He looked up at me with a peculiar look on his face and asked . . .'don't you want a see my driver's license and registration?' 'No', I replied, 'just be careful and try to stay out of trouble.' He looked at me and the look of love coming from him, was of course the Healing.

I took the Mark IV to a local body and fender repair shop, took $2,000. out of my savings to pay for the repair, a very tough thing for a nice Jewish boy from the Bronx to do and sold the car a few weeks later.

I never reported it to the police or the insurance company, nor did I dwell on my 'supposed' loss. That 'accident' was without a doubt the key to my being able to understand Lesson 1, which might just be the most difficult lesson, for all of us. It starts us in making the shift, the 360 degree shift, from what is not at all important, to what is most important. The most important lesson for us, is to recognize, that we must remain peaceful . . . no matter what. Or as Workbook Lesson 34 states . . .

'I could see peace instead of this.'

Not long after this incident occurred. I bought a Toyota (same color) which as I'm writing this book, I still drive and enjoy. The car has 125,000 miles on it and it has been trouble free and the best car I have ever owned.

With Spirit . . . there are no losers . . . only winners.

---

* Workbook Lesson #34, Book II, A Course in Miracles is published by the Foundation For Inner Peace, Glen Ellen, CA.

My Thoughts

Death Or Eternal Life

The more I learn about Jesus and his mission, the more convinced I become, that he came to teach us three major lessons. These lessons as I see it are:

1. Love . . . unconditionally
2. Forgiveness of everyone, no matter what
3. There is no death

It is the number 3. that I believe is most frightening to most of us and I know in my own life, my fear of dying, and dying young, was very much present. After all, my father died, a very young man. I was a witness to my mother's being ill with constant heart problems and around the time that my father decided to leave his body, several uncles and aunts, also made the same decision. I used to think and believe, that we had absolutely no control over, living or dying and that GOD was pulling the strings on us, like at a puppet show. It wasn't till I started to understand what Jesus was saying, that I started to change my thinking on this issue, regarding death and our reality . . . eternal life.

On page 217 in the Text Book I, Jesus says to us:

'When you are tempted to yield to the desire for death, remember that I did not die. You will realize that this is true when you look within and see me. Would I have overcome death for myself alone? And would eternal life have been given me of the Father unless He had also given it to you? When you learn to make me manifest, you will never see death. For you will have looked upon the deathless in yourself, and you will see only the eternal as you look out upon a world that cannot die.'

I believe that my fear of death and perhaps yours as well, becomes so frightening to us, early in life, because of our fear and our not knowing, where we're going. Most religions would have us believe, that if we behave ourselves, honor the Ten Commandments and throw a few dollars into the basket, that GOD will look upon us <u>favorably and</u> as soon as we die, we are on our way to Heaven. To

---

* Text Book I of A Course in Miracles, published by the Foundation For Inner Peace, Glen Ellen, CA.

stay forevermore in this wonderful place. Ah . . . but what about those of us that do some-not-so-very-nice things, what happens to us? I grew up believing that there was yet another place that we would make our final journey to and that was certainly another frightening prospect to live with.

In the time since I started to explore the possibilities, that some of this Wisdom that Jesus was giving to us, might possibly be true, one thing that is quite clear to me, is, that all of his teachings certainly make much more sense, than anything I was believing as my truth, before my involvement with the Course.

On Page 388, Book I, the Text, we are told:

'No one can die unless he chooses death.'

Twenty years ago, I would have asked the question, who in their right mind, would choose death? Today I understand this concept that we're asked to believe, that we choose and experience illness, only when we ask for and accept it and the very same thing applies to death, that we choose and experience death, only when we ask for it and accept it. My most sincere belief, right now, is, that we do not have to be sick and we do not need to die. Sickness and death is a decision that we make, believe it or not. The Course further reminds us that 'sickness is a defense against the truth.'

Is it not more comfortable to accept Jesus's teaching, that we are not being punished by GOD, when we get sick or 'seemingly' die but that we ourselves, are in some way, designing our own destinies in the illusion. We all seem to buy into what most people accept as their truth, that GOD is waiting for us to make one slip, one mistake, one error, so terrible that at the moment that mistake happens, GOD unleashes HIS vengeance against us and poof, we've got cancer, aids or a host of other horrible illnesses and then . . . the grim reaper . . . death. In my book, this book, I can tell you and I am telling you that none of our old beliefs, make any sense at all. I believe that Jesus's Message, that he came into this world of form to deliver is the Message that we finally have received in this and with this Course. I am reminded that there is a lovely passage that appears in The Song Of Prayer, Page 16, that comes from the same Source as the Course and the Psychotherapy Book, also dictated to Dr. Helen

---

*A Course In Miracles, The Song Of Prayer and Psycotherapy, Purpose, Process and Practice are both published by the Foundation For Inner Peace, Glen Ellen, CA.

Schuckman and printed by me in 1978, which states:

'This is what death should be; a quiet choice, made joyfully and with a sense of peace, because the body has been kindly used to help the son of GOD along the way he goes to GOD. We thank the body, then for all the service it has given us. But we are thankful, too, the need is done to walk the world of limits, and to reach the Christ in hidden form and clearly seen at most in lovely flashes. Now we can behold Him without blinders, in the light that we have earned to look upon again.

We call it death, but it is liberty. It does not come in forms that seem to be thrust down in pain upon unwilling flesh, but as a gentle welcome to release. If there has been true healing, this can be the form in which death comes when it is time to rest a while from labor gladly done and gladly ended . . Now we go in peace to freer air and gentler climate, where it is not hard to see the gifts we gave were saved for us. For Christ is clearer now; His vision more sustained in us; His Voice, the Word of GOD, more certainly our own.'

One of the definitions of death in Webster's Dictionary is: 'the lack of existence.' Can we accept that definition as our truth? I think not. The Holy Spirit and our elder brother Jesus has given us a far better definition.

My Thoughts

The Healing of Steven

A great many people that attend my lectures all over the country ask me how I can believe, so strongly, that all of these things that I talk about, have become my Truth. A great many of the concepts that I have written about in this book and that are mentioned in my lectures are to say the least, puzzling to many, confusing to some and downright unbelievable to others. I'm often questioned how I can believe all this 'stuff' I'm talking and writing about. Well since you've asked, I'll tell you:

Not too long after I completed the printing of A Course In Miracles, I was confronted by someone in my own family, who was going through, what he believed at that time, was a life threatening experience. The family member I'm referring to is my nephew Steven.

At the time this took place, Steven was, I believe about twenty three years of age and life up to this point, for Steven had been wonderful and at this time, Steven was working as a salesman, with his father in a somewhat elite men's clothing store and earning his living as a salesman and picking up a few extra bucks on weekends, by playing guitar and singing. Steven had met a lovely young woman named Laurie, at the store who served as cashier and a romance started to blossom. Everything was rolling along real well for a time, until Steven and Steven's mom and dad, noticed that Steven was starting to speak with a little bit of hoarseness, when he would speak or sing. His romance with Laurie was getting a little more serious and Steven's mom and dad were concerned, that Steven and Laurie were actually thinking about engagement and then marriage. This was not, I believe a very comfortable prospect for Steven's folks because Laurie was of a different religion and as with a great many Jewish people, marrying someone of a different faith is somewhat frowned upon.

Well anyway as Steven's romance got more and more serious, Steven's throat got more and more hoarse. It was frightening to say the least, to Steven and equally as frightening to Steven's parents and the decision was made to see a doctor immediately, upon seeing that the hoarseness was not 'going away'.

After examining Steven, the doctor told Steven and his parents that, what was causing the hoarseness in Steven's speech, was that Steven had developed twenty one growths in his throat, or as the doctor called them, papillomas. This of course frightened the you know what, out of Steven, Laurie and of course Steven's mom and dad. The doctor's advice was, that the growths had to be removed surgically and an appointment was made for surgery. The doctor cautioned everyone concerned that even with the removal of all twenty one papillomas, Steven would be left with a permanent hoarseness to his voice and I'm sure that the fear of what they all felt was yet another problem, to be dealt with.

Well the time of surgery had arrived and just before the effects of the ether was taking over, the surgeon found it necessary to lean down close to Steven's ear and say, there is a great deal, we do not know about these papillomas, but I'm going to go in as deep as I can, but there still remains the possibility, that they may grow back. The operation was completed, Steven went back to work with a very much lower voice and guess what? About three months later every single one of the growths were back in Steven's throat and again they were back in a doctor's office, this time a specialist, on Park Avenue in Manhattan. The specialist, while not wanting to appear unprofessional, told Steven and Steven's parents that unfortunately, the first surgeon had not 'gone deep enough' but that he would go deeper and get 'the root.' Unfortunately, this would leave Steven with a permanent disability, that being, that Steven would not be able to speak above a whisper, for the rest of his life. More fear . . . more guilt.

The second operation was scheduled and taking place and once again the new surgeon felt the necessity to caution and alert Steven to the possibility that even though he was 'going deeper and trying to get all of the root, of each growth' there still remained the possibility that the growths, could come back.

Once again the surgery being over, Steven tried going back to work, his voice hardly audible, but trying his best, somehow managed but singing was now definitely out of the question. His voice almost non existent and the fear was getting to everyone. Almost three months later . . . you guessed it, the growths were all back, every single one of the twenty one, back in all their glory. It appeared that these little suckers had a mind of their own and what it appeared that what they were doing, was defying, the skills and expertise of the surgeons. It seemed like the best thing that could be done would be to schedule a third surgery and by this time everyone concerned was convinced that Steven's growths were some new form of cancer and that his young life was soon to come to an end.

The search began for a third surgeon and by this time Steven was believing that he had cancer and that unless he had a third surgery there was every reason to believe that he would not survive. That's what he and the family was thinking, only one problem . . . Steven was totally opposed to being cut a third time and his objections were totally being ignored. This time a doctor who was using a new technique called 'lazer surgery' was found way up in Boston, Massachusetts and it was decided by Steven's mom and dad, that the surgery should take place in a few weeks and that this was the only path open for Steven's survival.

The problem was, that Steven was adamant about not going and refused to submit to a third surgery.

About this time Steven came to visit me in my office in Farmingdale, and we talked about what was going on and that he was not at all wanting to go for the lazer surgery and that he would rather go thru whatever time he had left, with the growths, in tact. He then said something to me, that I had never heard before and I quote: 'Uncle Sonny, I know that no one in this world has more weird friends than you have, is it at all possible that maybe one of those 'weird' friends of yours, could help me?' I looked at Steven, not really knowing what to say, or how to respond to his question and said, 'I'll make a few calls.'

The only person I knew of at that time, that I had heard was doing Healing through GOD, was Robert Skutch, who of course was, and is the man, along with his then wife Judy, was responsible for the publishing of A Course In Miracles and I had heard that he was having eight to ten people each night, to his home and actually talking to them about their problems. Somehow, I had heard, he was actually successful with some of these people who were coming and some of the people had actually had Healing.

I picked up the phone made my call to Bob and he invited me and Steven to his home and then added, bring Laurie as well. He requested that I not bring Steven's parents and at that time I had no

* A Course in Miracles is published by the Foundation For Inner Peace, Glen Ellen, CA.

idea, why. I picked Steven and Laurie up and the three of us were on our way into Manhattan and eighty first street and Central Park West. No traffic, and no trouble at all parking. We were announced by the now familiar doorman and when the elevator door opened, Bob was there to welcome the three of us and after taking our coats, ushered us into the living room and asked Steven to sit to the left of him on the couch and he asked me to sit on a chair opposite them and Laurie opposite me. Without any delay but not at all hurried, Bob looked at Steven and said that he was familiar with what had been going on thru what I had told him and that Steven's mom and dad had found a new surgeon. Bob asked Steven how he felt about going in for the third scheduled surgery and Steven replied . . . no way, was he willing to go under the knife a third time.

The atmosphere was calm, tranquil and relaxed and Bob then shot a question to Steven which caught us all off guard. The question was, 'Steve as a child, did you ever have warts? Steven looked at Bob, I looked at Bob, Laurie looked at Bob, all three of us wondering, what kind of question was that, with Steven facing possible death. Bob, very relaxed, asked, 'well did you?' Steven started to think and after a few moments answered, 'well yes, I guess I did'. Bob never losing eye contact, gently then asked, 'Steve could you show me, just where those warts were? Steven, very much puzzled by the question, looked down at his hands, lifted both hands off of his lap and seemed to be studying where those warts were. Slowly, starting with his left hand, he pointed with his right hand and said, 'well I think I had one here, pointing to the pinky of his left hand, and then there was one here, pointing to the next finger on his left hand and across his left hand pointing out where he was remembering, the location of his warts. Then he switched hands, now using his left hand to point out the location of the warts on his right hand, Steven repeated the process and after pointing out where the warts were, looked up at Bob. Bob then asked 'Steve, where are all those warts now?' Puzzled, Steven again glanced down at his fingers, slowly examining both hands, looked back up at Bob and replied . . . 'they're gone'. Bob moving his head in a 'yes' motion said, 'yes Steve, they're gone'. Neither Bob nor Steven said anything for the next twenty seconds and it was as if time was being allowed to allow the discovery that the warts were no longer clinging to Steven's fingers.

Bob then said, Steve those growths in your throat are exactly the same as the warts you had on your fingers as a kid, which are 'all gone, at this time'. He continued, 'just as you got rid of your warts, you can get rid of those growths. Have you asked GOD for help?' Steven answered, 'well I believe I did, but can you help me to ask GOD, again?' Bob smiled and said, 'sure Steve, let's go into the bedroom and ask GOD'S help'. They both got up, walked towards the bedroom, closed the door behind them and were gone. The moment the door closed, Laurie leaned over towards me and whispered, 'what are they doing?' I leaned over towards her and whispered back, 'I don't have the vaguest idea, what they're doing'.

About five minutes went by and the door to the bedroom opened and Steven and Bob walked out, both smiling and Bob said 'don't worry Steve, it's in GOD'S Hands now, everything will be fine.' He gave us our coats and said 'by the way Steve, stop trying to please everyone else and go for your own happiness and peace of mind. If you love this gal, marry her, and don't let anyone change your mind about your decision. Your peace and happiness, is up to you.

As Steven, Laurie and I got into the elevator both Laurie and I were bursting to find out what had happened in the bedroom and as soon as the elevator started down, Laurie burst out and questioned, 'well tell us already, what happened in the bedroom?' Steven still looking and feeling quite peaceful, slowly answered, it was amazing, 'Bob put his fingers on my throat and we asked GOD together, to help me to get rid of these growths in my throat and all of a sudden I started to feel electricity coming out of the end of Bob's fingers, it was GOD sending electricity thru Bob's fingers to me.' It was amazing. Laurie looked at me, I looked at Laurie and both of us were thinking the same thing . . . this is most definitely weird.

As we got into my car, I figured that both of these kids had just been exposed to a 'somewhat unusual experience' and I thought about what we should do now and I decided to do what any Jewish uncle with his Jewish nephew and Gentile sweetheart should do . . . I took them for Chinese food. In the restaurant we spoke about Steven's experience and I said, 'you know Steve, it sounded like Bob's advice to you, made a lot of sense. I know that you, wanting to be a dutiful son, are being pulled one way as far as your relationship with Laurie is concerned, and I also recognize that you are pulling yourself in the opposite direction, because you seem to love Laurie very much and I guess the result is a kind of tug of war, within yourself. Maybe these growths have something to do with your seeming inability to talk up for what you truly believe you should do with this relationship and perhaps this is your mind's way of showing protest, within your body'. Steven replied, 'maybe'.

I drove the kids back to Long Island, dropped them off at Steven's folk's home and continued East to my house and went to sleep wondering about, what I had just witnessed.

About two weeks later, Steven had a most unusual experience. As he, his sister, mom and dad were eating dinner Steven started to gag and feeling a somewhat foreign substance in his throat, brought up this substance. He took this ball shaped bit of what he thought was something in his food, placed it in the palm of his hand, examined it for a moment and what he saw was a perfectly round piece of skin, pinkish in color and appearing like a small marble. He said to his family, hey, mom, dad, look what I just coughed up. Everyone at the table was mystified, including Steven, as they had no idea, what Steve had just coughed up. The specialist, who had performed the second surgery, was called and when they told him what had just happened, the doctor, said you'd better come in immediately. All four people, Steve, mom, dad and Steve's sister thought the worst, that Steve's throat was coming apart and a very worried group found themselves on the way into Manhattan, fearing the worst.

The doctor looked at this flesh colored object and then asked Steve if he could look into Steve's throat. He looked into Steve's throat using that apparatus that doctors use when examining throats and ears, turned around to Steve and his parents and said, 'this is amazing, he repeated, this is amazing.' He then said 'what Steve had coughed up was one of the twenty one growths, that had been removed twice surgically, and had grown back'. What astounded the doctor was that the growth that Steve had coughed up was perfectly rounded and the spot where that growth had been, appeared to be perfectly healed, showing no scar tissue from either of the two operations and as far as the doctor could tell, it was like that growth, was never there. The doctor sat down and asked Steve to tell him exactly what had happened since the second operation that he had performed and Steven recounted the entire story to the doctor, including my taking him and Laurie to Bob's home and thru sitting down at dinner and coughing up this growth. The doctor scratched his head, mentioned that in all his years of doctoring and surgery, he had never encountered anything like this before and he said, 'Steve, I don't know how this could happen, but if I were you, I'd keep doing exactly, whatever it is, you are doing. I just don't understand the whole thing'.

The third surgery was canceled and within the next two and one half months, the other twenty growths came out of Steve's throat, precisely, the same way, the first growth had come out. All twenty one, had come out, the same color, the same size, the same way.

For me, the thing that was so amazing was that Steve's voice, which just a few months earlier, had been hardly audible was now back and I had no difficulty in hearing him, when he spoke. His voice was back. He resumed his life and oh yes . . . he married Laurie and they are now, some fourteen years later, still married, quite happy and very much in love.

The growths have never come back Steven had a Healing thru GOD, the only Healing, that truly exists.

My Thoughts

Special Love Relationships

The Course tells us that we (the world) use our special love relationships as a final weapon of exclusion and a demonstration of separateness and that the Holy Spirit transforms them into perfect lessons in forgiveness and in awakening us from the dream. Each lesson or special relationship is an opportunity to let our perception be healed and our errors corrected. Most importantly it presents us with yet another chance to forgive oneself by forgiving the other and each experience or relationship yet becomes another opportunity to invite the Holy Spirit and GOD into the experience.

Have you ever wondered why two people who are madly in love one day, can be absolutely furious with each other, the next day. The special love, has turned into special hate. Our projection, or the way we see things, take two different forms, they are special love and special hate. When we feel guilty, we feel uncomfortable with the guilt and want to get rid of the guilt any way and as quickly as we can, so we transfer the guilt to someone else, thus we feel more comfortable. Our thinking becomes, why should we feel uncomfortable or miserable, we project it on to someone else and they are responsible for whatever misery we are feeling, puff . . . we once again feel good. The special love, in an instant, or in a year, or in a lifetime, has become special hate.

Somehow or another, we start to believe that someone else can take care of our needs and we start to believe that our special needs, can be taken care of, by special people, with special qualities . . . sooo . . . the special love takes on a sort of dependency . . . on someone else. The Course clearly teaches us that no one else is responsible for our peace or happiness as that has been given and guaranteed to us by GOD. Yet we all feel this dependency, that some other person is responsible, for our happiness and well being. Seeing someone else as 'more special' than someone else, indicates that you or them, are 'not equals' or that GOD created one of us with more to offer, more to give, or having more. This is not the case since GOD is an equal opportunity Father. Each and every one of us receive the exact same thing from our Father. In short, when you are ready to give up the whole concept of specialness, at that moment you are set free.

*A Course in Miracles is published by the Foundation For Inner Peace, Glen Ellen, CA.

Seeing your mother, your father, your sister, your brother, your husband, your wife, your sweetheart, your lover, your uncles, your aunts, your cousins, your friends as special, is not the Truth.

So how do we get out of this feeling of specialness, which in the truest sense, separates us from one another, the Course tells us thru Forgiveness. That's right Forgiveness.

On Page 470 in the Text, Book I, The Course tells us that,

'Forgiveness is the end of specialness'.

It is emphasized that our peace comes only from this Forgiveness and if that there was not condemnation, there would be no need for Forgiveness. I have stated earlier in this book, that GOD never condemns, GOD never punishes . . . therefore GOD has no need to Forgive us for anything that we think we may have done, simply because GOD cannot create anything imperfect. Since we are GOD'S creation, we are in the truest sense . . . absolutely perfect. We just have not accepted this fact as our truth, as yet. How can one perfect, be more perfect, than another. How can one perfect seek or find the need to find their perfection, in another's perfection. The answer is, that we can't. When you can no longer see sin, in anyone, you will be at total peace.

I have stated that in the illusion, the big dream, when it comes to its end, each and everyone of us, without exception, will see the Christ, or the Light, in each and every one of us, also without exception, and that we will all be participating and practicing 'Unconditional Love', and then and only then, is the illusion over. No one of us is . . . more special . . . than the other. This can only happen, when not a single one of us, the beautiful children of a Loving Father, in whom He is well pleased, can see and accept, in each and everyone of us the Truth, that not one of us is more special than any other one of us.

---

* *A Course in Miracles is published by the Foundation For Inner Peace, Glen Ellen, CA.*

Depression

My father's death certificate read that a coronary thrombosis led to his leaving his body. I don't agree, I believe it was depression. For as long as I can remember, before his body died, my father always enjoyed the best of health and I can't remember him ever losing a days work or pay at the job he held for thirty three years. The job he held for so long, was that of plant superintendent at a fairly large printing plant called, Pacific Printing, located at 37 East 18th Street, in Manhattan.

During the thirty three years, that he ran this plant, the thing that stands out most in my mind, was his dreaming about his retiring, on his union pension and going down to Florida, to live out his remaining years. There was not a day that passed, that my father didn't mention his Florida dream and since we worked together, lived together, rode the bus together and took the subway together, I got to hear more about that dream, than anyone else.

What I didn't know at that time was that my father would never realize his dream of the future in Florida, since he was going to leave his body, at the age of fifty five, seven years before his planned retirement.

With never a hint or clue of what was about to happen, after thirty three years on the same job, with the same firm, in the same capacity, my father was told that the firm he had spent so many years with, was about to change hands. Things were not going well financially for Pacific Printing and the decision was made that Pacific Printing would be merged with Stuyvesant Press, a much newer and financially more successful company. Since Stuyvesant Press had their own personnel, both workers and supervisory, it was decided that all or most of the workers from Pacific would be integrated into the ranks of Stuyvesant's personnel and my father was, of course, asked to remain in precisely the same type of work, he had been performing, all of those years . . . with just one tiny difference, that difference being, that he no longer had the title of plant superintendent.

For some reason, his ego portion of mind, saw this as a demotion of sorts and suddenly in his thinking, a fear set in, that his lifestyle was being threatened, that this was a demotion, that his age was a factor, but the most serious thing that this merger was doing to him personally, was that his 'dream' was being threatened. I remember well that he suddenly, started experiencing difficulty with his eye sight and he started to blame his glasses. The prescription was strengthened and still there was difficulty. Then I noticed something new starting to happen. Since I lived one floor above where my mother and father lived in an apartment in Yonkers, New York, it was my custom to drop in and chat with mom and dad, see if they needed anything etc. One evening, soon after the 'merger' was announced, I came in to the apartment and found my father sitting in his favorite easy chair, totally in the dark, blankly staring off into space. It seemed to me as if his mind had completely gone blank and that the answer to his question of 'why', was somewhere out there in space.

This was of course, many years before my involvement with the Course or the Course Psychotherapy and Attitudinal Healing and I had no idea, what he was doing to himself.

This silent staring out into space continued for about a year and one morning, as usual, we went to work together and on the subway, Dad complained about a pain he had experienced in his right arm, throughout the night. As he shared this news of his discomfort with me, the only thing I could think of to say was, 'oh, you probably caught a draft in your arm, during the night and that it would disappear, once he got to work.'

That day the pain did not disappear, once he got to work and as a matter of fact, the pain increased, more and more as the day went on and for the very first time in thirty three years on the job, my father left the job early and went home . . . to 'die'.

When I got home that evening, I was met by a woman who lived in the building, who gave me the news that my father had died, and when I entered Mom and Dad's apartment and saw mom's face, I didn't have be told that the news, was true. I remember sitting down on his bed, next to his body, and with tears running down my cheeks, asking, why . . . why . . . why?

Here was a man who was never sick a day in his life, who I observed enjoying perfect health, all of the years I was growing up, and suddenly without any kind of warning, he was no longer here in body. What had happened? Why, with everything going so well,

*A Course In Miracles and Psycotherapy, Purpose, Process and Practice, published by the Foundation For Inner Peace, Glen Ellen, CA.

would he leave? It took me many years to figure the whole thing out and it was only after I started to understand the Course, the Psychotherapy and Attitudinal Healing, that any of this made any sense, at all.

Somehow my father s sense of self esteem, self worth, was not threatened at all, while he was working as plant superintendent at Pacific Printing all those thirty three years. He placed himself in a state of being, making himself happy, secure and feeling that he was fulfilling a role of leadership, with much responsibility as a leader. Suddenly his security and his dream were threatened and he started to think that his age, was a factor in what seemed to be happening to him. Suddenly he started to believe and accept that his body, was failing him. His ego thought system had convinced him that he was less of a person, in every way and as we know, the ego can only demonstrate through the body. His dream of Florida was definitely in his thinking, in jeopardy. Negative thoughts had invaded his thinking and for the first time in his life, he was frightened, confused and a sense of futility was most definitely present. This is depression, make no mistake about it.

With depression, the confusion, the fear, the uncertainty and the futility take over our thinking and suddenly our life itself, is most surely threatened. In Dr. David R. Hawkins, Map of Consciousness, he shows the levels of death, the emotions that are surely present are:

death . . . the view of life . . . . hopeless
death . . . the level of consciousness . . . . apathy
death . . . the emotion . . . . hopelessness/despair
death . . . the process . . . . de-energized

destroyers . . sin . . . guilt . . . self hate . . ultimately destruction

Now if I've learned anything at all with my years with the Course, Psychotherapy and Attitudinal Healing, it is without a doubt, that none of our problems, create themselves, we are their creators. Take heart, since all of the problems that we create are not for the sake of punishments but are for our own learning experiences. I have accepted that those that we choose to be in a special love or even a special hate relationship with, are most definitely our teachers as we are theirs. My father was a marvelous teacher for me and his role in my life is quite clear to me, at this time. Not only did he teach

---

*A Course In Miracles and Psycotherapy, Purpose, Process and Practice, published by the Foundation For Inner Peace, Glen Ellen, CA.
* Dr. Hawkins Map of Consciousness is available at no cost through Mind and Miracles, Ft. Lauderdale, FL.

me to become a printer, a good father and a man, he also was a good friend and parent who gave me his love, his trust and most importantly, my belief in GOD. He taught me about life and living and he also taught me about death and dying.

Along with my elder brother Jesus, my father was a marvelous teacher to me, teaching me the lesson that there is no death, or what we perceive as death is merely, as Jesus puts it, 'is the quiet laying down of the body after it has fulfilled it's purpose, as a teaching device'.

Yes, it was Jesus that taught me 'that there is no death,' but it was my father who taught me, that we don't die. You see he is very much alive, even though his body no longer exists, as Jesus and all of us are, since we are able to communicate whenever we wish. No my father who taught me so much, never made it to Florida for retirement but he did make retirement, nevertheless, to a far better place.

Diets Don't Work, Try . . . With Every Bite, I'm Getting Light

I was born the son of a set of parents who were both overweight and loved to eat. For most of my life, I figured the reason that I was overweight was due to their being overweight. As a young child, I felt embarrassed because I was the heaviest child in my class in school. I can remember wishing that I could be old enough to eat my meals in restaurants and dreamed that when I was old enough to select other foods, than the foods I was then eating, I would surely become slim, trim and the perfect weight for my height. If that could only happen I thought, I would be a much happier person and the embarrassment, would totally disappear.

It didn't help much, that my mother was a fabulous cook and that her greatest joy seemed to be the huge meals she prepared, which were always lovingly prepared, filled with all kinds of delicious, delectable 'goodies' and loaded with hundreds of thousand of calories. While going to public school, my lunch every day for the entire time spent in public school and coming home at twelve o'clock, for lunch, consisted of, two fried eggs on kaiser rolls (seeded if you please), smothered in ketchup and a tall glass of milk, with two freshly baked jelly doughnuts. With the one block walk back to school, it hardly gave me the opportunity to work off, or walk off, any portion of the meal.

Dinner at the Steinberg residence was another matter, as my mother believed that every dinner meal required being cooked, served and eaten as a sort of banquet, which usually consisted of, the appetizer, then the soup, the meat (every night a different cut), with at least one type of potato, at least two vegetables, rye bread and butter, soda or beer, to drown the whole thing down . . . and then the specialty of the evening, the large bowl of fruit and the baked desert. Ah, the deserts. As mentioned, my mother was not only a fabulous cook, she was also a fabulous baker and her baked specialties, were without equal . . . her 'rugelach' was known all over the East Bronx and when she baked, which was often, people came from all over the Bronx, it seemed and crowded into our house to share her 'goodies'.

Remembering back to those days, 1 guess what amazes me

most, is my brother Stanley, who out ate me, mom and dad, stayed slim and trim, despise the huge meals he consumed and as I examine this curious phenomenon, I can only think he knew more meta-physically at that time, than the rest of us.

I remember after basic training in the army, that I slimmed down to a thirty six inch waist. I thought at that time the losing of the extra weight was due to the regimen of heavy duty marching, hiking and exercises and most definitely getting away from 'mamma's cooking' and I stayed fairly trim, the two years I spent in Fort Knox, Kentucky.

About a year after being discharged from the army, I married my lovely wife Judy and introduced her to my mother's cooking and it did not take long for both of us to start shopping for jumbo sizes and the days of our being slim and trim, seemed to be over. In the next several years, our three children, Paul, Linda and Sandi, were born and I guess Judy and I, not wanting them to run into the same weight problems, cut out salt, butter, eggs and meat and while our weight remained the same, the three kids, stayed slim and trim. About this time, the media seemed to really be coming down on the issues and dangers of obesity, high blood pressure and one's dying before one's time. These messages, I was sure, were all aimed at me and since there was a history of all these problems and it seemed that early dying and heart problems ran in my family, I better do something about all that 'fat around my heart' and everywhere else, on my body, before I became a statistic and my children were to be robbed of their father.

The time to do something about 'my fat', had arrived and I enrolled myself into a program at the local 'Y', where I had to undergo a stress test, a thorough doctor's examination and my blood had to 'check out', before I or anyone else was permitted to participate. Believing that I was an athletic type, I did fairly well on the treadmill portion of the stress test and the doctor seemed rather surprised that a man with all those extra pounds, hanging on to him, could and did show such a strong endurance. I did not do nearly as well with the blood test and my blood showed an elevated (as the doctor put it) high triglycerides, high blood sugar, high cholesterol and high blood pressure. The doctor told me that I had two choices, to take these four 'highs' down. My choices were, (1) to go on medication, (not meditation) for the rest of my life, which he didn't feel was going to be for very long, or, (2) a vigorous exercise and diet program.

I opted for choice number (2), as I had seen my mother swallow enough pills in her life and I had observed, that with all of the pills she had taken, there seemed to be no change in her condition, or did her heart problems improve.

I started the program at the 'Y' with my slim partner, Len Coleman. The program consisted of going to the 'Y' three mornings per week, plus Saturday, for sports. We jogged, exercised and played racquetball all four mornings and 'oh yes', we also went for giant breakfasts after all four sessions and buffet lunches (the all you can eat kind) at nearby restaurants. Len got slimmer and I got even fatter.

By this time, and we're talking about the late 1970's, I had already printed A Course In Miracles and my cousin and teacher, Paul Steinberg, came to my office one day and he invited me to join him for lunch. Paul also perceived that he had a weight problem but the first thing that I noticed, was that he appeared to be somewhat slimmer. We went to the restaurant next door to my quickprint and I ordered my usual sandwich and cup of coffee. Paul ordered a hamburger with fries, a chocolate malted and a piece of strawberry short cake. Before taking his first bite, I noticed that Paul closed his eyes for a couple of moments and I thought he was saying some kind of Grace, before eating. I watched my cousin down the entire meal, with disbelief, and I asked 'if he always ate like that' and he replied that these days, he did and then he added, 'that's how I'm losing my weight. I looked at him and said, 'come on Paul, you're putting me on aren't you'? No Spank, he answered, 'I've lost sixty pounds, eating like this'. I asked Paul what his secret was and he answered 'did you notice my short meditation, before we started eating?' I said, 'yes I but I thought you were saying Grace'. 'No', he replied, 'I was repeating a kind of a mantra that I've been using for several months now and it works'. I asked, 'ok, what's the mantra?' He looked at me, smiled and said 'with every bite I'm getting Light'. I looked at my crazy cousin, who had lured and pulled me through many strange experiences and asked, 'what the hell is that?' Still smiling, he answered, 'that it was an old metaphysical axiom, that

* A Course in Miracles is published by the Foundation For Inner Peace, Glen Ellen, CA.

really works. In other words, he explained, 'you simply take the power, away from the foods that you eat, that power that you have given, to the foods that you eat, by allowing your Mind to order your body, not to allow whatever you eat, or, how much you eat, or, the feared weight gain, to happen. I looked at Paul and thought to myself, once again, this time he's really flipped, but I could not deny the fact that he looked slim and trim. I asked if that was all there was to it and he answered, 'no, one also had to do a visualization technique'.

Once again, feeling that I was being drawn into one of Paul's nutty beliefs, I asked feeling rather foolish, 'what is a visualization technique?' Paul answered, 'close your eyes as you are saying, with every bite, I'm getting Light and form in your thinking, a mental picture of yourself as slim as you wish yourself, to be. Simple as that, do it each and every time you put anything in your mouth, regardless, of what it is, or, how often and the weight will come of as quickly as you wish it to do so. This is how I have lost my sixty pounds and was able to eat everything I love to eat'. There was no doubt in my mind, that Paul had most definitely lost it, his mind that is, this time, but I was seeing a slimmed down Paul Steinberg, but this was definitely to far out for me in 1977.

A short time later Spirit brought Dr. David Hawkins into my life and as I've mentioned earlier in this book, he became a wonderful teacher to me and many others. In the video series, 12 Office Visits With The Good Doctor, that we did together, the second video dealing with weight not only discussed Paul's concepts and theories but also added many new and most exciting ways on losing weight through the Mind. The message on that video is simply, that only the Power of the GOD Mind can help you to let go of the belief that food of any description has any power over us, and that no foods can make us heavier or obese, unless we give it the power to do so. Further that diets, any diets, definitely do not work and that the billions of dollars that have been spent so far, is equal to taking your money and throwing it down the toilet.

Once Judy and I started to accept the concepts, that Dave shares with us on this tape, the weight on both of us, started to come off, day by day, month by month. It has now been more than eight years, since making that video tape and I must tell you that for a man who

---

* *12 Office Visits With The Good Doctor is a set of 12 Video Tapes produced by Mind and Miracles, Ft. Lauderdale, FL.*

up until eight years ago, probably lost and then gained back thousands of pounds, this is the first time in my life that I have not gained a back single pound, after losing, the initial weight that I programmed my Mind, to get rid of, to help me lose. I have not gotten on a scale, in the past eight years and eat anything and everything, I feel like eating and there are absolutely no restrictions. People who knew me back in the years before my discovering this most unique method of Attitudinal Healing, concerning weight, are constantly amazed that I look so different, than I used to. I was a forty seven inch waist when I was struggling to lose those unwanted pounds, and after applying the principals that Paul and Dave helped me to learn, I went down to my present waistline, which is a thirty seven inch waistline and this has been accomplished totally without dieting, or taking any pills and as mentioned earlier, I have not been in a doctor's office, or 'checked up' since the stress test mentioned earlier in this chapter, which took place in 1974.

Judy has experienced the very same results and in her case, she has gone from a size sixteen, down to her present size of being an eleven. We both have been able to enjoy any and all foods, that we love and although both of our tastes have changed, with things that we eat, we both feel that 'changing our minds, about weight and the foods that add or lose weight, on us, is strictly something that our minds have created. Neither of us has any fear of eating so called fattening foods, nor do we count calories, nor do we have any belief at all, that illness, any illness, due to our weight, can in any way, shape or form, be a factor that can or will, create any form of illness. For those of you that read this and might want to give these methods a try, I can only share with you, what Dr. Hawkins says on the video, and that is, that 'diets, no diets work' and that in order to reverse any negative condition, you must first change your mind, as to how you are accepting that condition.

Give it a try, you have nothing to lose . . . except perhaps some unwanted weight.

Remember, 'with every bite, I'm getting Light'.

My Thoughts

Self Esteem . . . Self Respect

In talking with my friend Henry, the subject of self respect, self esteem came up. To my knowledge, I have never given either of these two terms all that much thought, but now as I'm thinking about what makes some of us, go one way and others of us, go quite another way, I have come to the conclusion that perhaps these two terms (and that's all they are), have a great deal to do with our quality of life. What we perceive about ourselves and others indeed play a part, in our Healing process.

A Course In Miracles tells us that the one truth that never changes, is that we, every single one of us, again, without exception, are beautiful children of a Loving Father/Mother GOD, in whom She/He, is well pleased. If you think this fact of Life has been repeated and repeated and repeated in this book, you are absolutely correct. It's the most important thing in this book. But back to the topic. So why do we encounter so much difficulty in accepting this fact . . . as our truth. How and why should we feel great one moment and really low, the next moment? Most likely, the answer to that question, is fear. It starts with fear, it continues with fear and in many cases, ends with fear.

In the introduction to the Course, we are introduced to a 'new' logic, which tells us, *'that the opposite of love, is fear'*. This usually shocks most people when they first pick up the Course, as we've all been taught that the opposite of love is hate. What is hate but just another form of fear?

Getting back to Henry, this morning, Henry's wife Irene, a friend of Judy's and mine for many years, rushed into her kitchen, while Henry and I were having one of our most wonderful talks and Irene proclaimed, 'Oh GOD, I'm running late for work'. She appeared to be in a state of great agitation as many of us get when things don't go exactly as we've planned, or desire.

Henry and I were still talking, after Irene had hastily kissed Henry goodby and I said to Henry that Irene appeared to be putting herself under a great deal of stress and that her fear of being late, was in itself, more dangerous to Irene than the actuality of really being late. Now I don't know if Irene has been late getting to her job, once, twice, or a thousand times, but enough fear was present in what I

* Introduction to A Course in Miracles, Book I, published by the Foundation For Inner Peace, Glen Ellen, CA.
* A Course In Miracles is published by the Foundation For Inner Peace, Glen Ellen, CA.

observed in Irene, that I felt the need to ask, why was Irene so stressed? Henry told me that Irene's company, a very large well known Fortune 500 Company, due to the recession and economic problems, was on a drive to get rid of people and was making an issue of lateness and absenteeism. It occurred to me that here was an issue, which started with fear (the fear of being reprimanded, the fear of dismissal, the fear of not having the money, needed to pay the bills), which ultimately leads to a feeling somehow or another, of low self respect, which of course is also low self esteem. Somehow in our ego thinking, the idea, the belief, that we don't measure up, for whatever reasons we make up, we start to come down on ourselves for absolutely no reason. Without really thinking about any situation at all, it seems that we can be triggered by a random thought or even a comment from someone else, and in a split second, we can go from a place of peace, to a place of chaos, or even attack. Somehow our sense of self esteem/self worth figures into this whole crazy business.

So, our self esteem/self worth, as far as I'm concerned, boils down to how we conduct and handle ourselves. Whose voice do we choose to listen to? Spirit's or ego's? It also appears to me that once we get our self esteem/self worth working correctly, we are truly on the correct road to remembering our 'real' identity, and who we truly are. And so, it is clearly our sense of self worth/self esteem that provides us with this beautiful term we keep talking about which is our 'Inner Peace'. I have come to believe that it is impossible to be peaceful, if we do not have a 'real' sense of Spiritual Self Esteem and Self Worth. The Course tells us that we are all children of GOD and that by virtue of our birthright, we are automatically guaranteed to be no less than Perfect, Holy and completely without fault. That's right every single last one of us, without you know what (exception). Face it my brothers and sisters . . . we are Perfect.

In order to start that change of perception, we need to start, like now. We have to recognize our true identity, our strengths, our perfection and our Self Esteem/Self Worth. As a parent myself, as I'm sure many of you reading this book are, I often feel the urge to guide, correct and help my children when I see them painting themselves into a painful corner, where their self esteem/self worth is concerned. Why can't they see it as I do? I guess the reason is that they, as we, have to climb their own ladder as you and I have. We have all come into these bodies for a magnificent learning experience, which we all must take, in our own good time, or most likely, GOD'S Good Time.

My Thoughts

You're In The Army Now.

The question that many of us have is . . . is life in someway planned? Is there a script that we somehow follow . . . or . . . do we just plot along not really knowing at any level whether we are being guided by our ego mind or GOD Mind, or is every event in our life . . . a result of luck, of chance, or perhaps a combination of both. When I was twelve and one half years of age, I had been listening to my mother and father argue constantly about the same issue for twelve and one half years . . . and maybe even before that . . . while I was in my mother's womb. The arguments were always about the same subject . . . money. This constant arguing about money matters by Mom and Dad, even as a young child, seemed to be for me a pattern with my parents, which seemed to happen on a fairly regular basis. It probably had a great deal to do with forming my character as a person who needed to discover a way of earning my own way at an early age.

When I was twelve and one half years of age, after listening to Mom and Dad bickering about money matters, it just seemed more comfortable not to ask for an allowance, or even for clothing. My mother hounded Dad to get me a part time job at his place of employment, where he happened to be the plant superintendent, a printing concern called Pacific Printing Company, located on Eighteenth Street in Manhattan. Each day after school I would get on the IRT subway at 149th Street in the Bronx and take the subway into Manhattan, getting off at the 18th Street station in Manhattan. I never realized at the time that this part time job, with my Dad breaking me into his and his father's trade, was probably the reason I had chosen to incarnate into this particular family. It also gave me the opportunity, for the first time in this life, to earn my own way. I think the minimum wage per hour at that time was perhaps seventy-five cents an hour and while I was only able to work two or three hours per day, on Friday when we got our pay envelopes, to a twelve and a half year old from the Bronx it seemed like a great deal of money.

My father's plan for me was to serve an apprenticeship in The New York Typographical Union . . . called in those days, The Big Six and since there was already a man who was serving his apprenticeship my turn would not come up for some six or seven years down the road. I should have realized that something was being planned for me, when for the first several months of work with my father he and I were to proofread four different versions, in four different languages of the new testament for The New York Bible Society. At that time, I didn't believe that I understood one single word of what I was reading to my father and perhaps I still don't, but that was most certainly my very first meeting with my elder brother Jesus and my very first assignment in the printing trade.

I worked with my father at Pacific Printing all through Junior High School 52 and then continued all through James Monroe High School. Even after my graduation from High School I continued to work and waited patiently for the long awaited apprenticeship into The New York Typographical Union, which my father believed . . . would guarantee me a solid secure financial future. But alas . . . Spirit had other plans for me.

Precisely three months before I was to sign my name on the dotted line for the long awaited apprenticeship, I got a notice in the mail from my local draft board, that stated that I was needed to help my country fight the police action, as they called it, in Korea. My father was really devastated by my draft notice and I guess he truly believed that my long awaited guaranteed future, was going down the toilet and in addition to that, he also started to think that there was a chance that I might never return from Korea. He asked me to go to the draft board on Arthur Avenue in the Bronx to ask, to beg if need be, for a three month extension or deferment, so that I could at least sign my name to the apprenticeship papers, which would officially give me the apprenticeship and allow time served while in the Army, count towards my full apprenticeship. The draft board turned me down flat, telling me I was needed and that the war would seriously be jeopardized, if I wasn't in it.

On January 5th, 1952 my father drove me to Whitehall Street in lower Manhattan at 5:30 A M. to get on a bus which was going to transport me and a bus full of other inductees, to a place in New Jersey, called Camp Kilmer. It was cold, grey and not very cheerful. After four miserable days in Camp Kilmer, we were put on a train bound for Kentucky. The train ride seemed extra long and at about 3:30 A.M. the train pulled into a railroad station on the outskirts of

Louisville, Kentucky and I remember there was a brass band there, an Army Band, complete with yellow laces in their boots and yellow scarfs around their necks. This was our official welcome to Fort Knox and it was the first and last cordial event the United States Army would grant to any of us.

Since Fort Knox was the home of the Third Armored Division, I and everyone else were assigned to a company, whose assignment was to learn how to drive an M-47 tank. The tanks were newly designed and the 16 week basic training was of course, learning all about driving these huge machines. The rumor and most probably the truth was, that the North Koreans had figured out a way of killing tank drivers quickly and efficiently by planting a new type of land mine, which when driven over, would explode and blow the bottom hatch of the tank, up into the driver's face, which was rumored to in some way sever the driver's head, from the rest of his body. It dawned on me that this was not a very safe place to spend the next two years of my life and that a guy could get seriously hurt, in a place like Korea.

Being a Scorpio, I quickly discovered, that there was life beyond the tanks, in the nearby town of Louisville and started going into town on a fairly regular basis. The object was to meet anyone I could who would provide me with female company. One night I met a lovely lady and we proceeded to have a rather passionate evening. So passionate in fact that I overslept and missed reveille by about two hours. This was serious business during a war, even if it was called a police action and by the time I got back to Fort Knox, the court martial papers were already being prepared for Colonel Stuffelbeam. Shortly thereafter, the court martial did take place and I remember standing in front of Colonel Stuffelbeam, his voice stern and unwavering thundered . . . "Steinberg, I'm going to make an example of you. I'm going to find the worst job in this man's army and nail your ass to the barnyard door". . . as he put it.

A day or two later I was again summoned to appear in front of him and he told me that he had indeed located just such a terrible place befitting my behind. It turned out to be a place called The Training Literature and Reproduction Plant . . . a printing plant. The dirtiest job in this man's army turned out to be that of a plate grainer. It was certainly the loudest job I had ever encountered, up to that time. The object was to take previously used litho plates' very large litho plates and actually sand off the previous image. There was a huge pool table type of device, which you fastened the plate to, then the operator (me) would open a trap door, which would release what appeared to be and sounded like 10,000 steel ball bearings, along with a mixture of a sand like substance. The table would then electrically rotate at a very slow speed . . . thus removing the previous image off of the litho plate. The noise was absolutely deafening and it was clear to me that Colonel Stuffelbeam, perhaps in a previous lifetime had been that person during the Inquisition who had the job of stretching people on the rack. In order to survive plate graining I went to the PX and invested in cotton, but that didn't help. The next thing I did was to buy a set of ear plugs and they worked much better. I figured that if I had to spend the next two years in the plate graining room, I would no doubt go deaf, but I would also go crazy.

One day after about 2 weeks of plate graining, I walked over to the other side of this huge Training and Literature and Reproduction Plant and I spotted two Linotype machines, very much like I had worked on, before being drafted. Neither machine was operating and I asked a civilian man standing near by, why the machines were not on. He replied that for the past two years he had been looking for an operator, as he was the man in charge of the entire operation. He told me that for the past two years, in order to get the type needed for running this giant plant, he had to go all the way to Louisville, some 35 miles away, which was proving to be a real pain. I quickly volunteered to him that I could operate those Linotype machines and he looked at me, like I was Jesus, sent to him from heaven. He asked me to show him what I could do with the Linotypes and 20 minutes later my official job in the United States Army became that of printer.

My life had most definitely been turned in another direction as most of my outfit had indeed been sent to Korea and quite a few of the men I trained with, were indeed killed. I was being saved for some special assignment but at that time way back in 1952. I had absolutely no idea what that assignment was to be.

Holy Spirit did know . . . I was needed, to become the printer of A Course In Miracles, some twenty three years later. The script

* A Course in Miracles is published by the Foundation For Inner Peace, Glen Ellen, CA.

was most definitely being prepared . . . and . . . those of us who were chosen, for our parts . . . were most definitely, assigned our roles.

My Thoughts

Bershart . . Meant To Be . . Karma

For most of my life, before my involvement with Course In Miracles, I believed in the five words which title this page. The word bershart (a yiddish word) loosely translated means that any event, good or bad, when it happens, was meant to be. That no matter what that particular event turns out to be, that nothing, absolutely nothing, could change the outcome of that event. The meant to be statement is just that. It is stating that somehow when that particular event happens, it is suggesting that some heavenly power, maybe even GOD, is ordaining, that nothing could possibly change, that event, which must happen. The fifth word is a word that I first heard, when I started printing metaphysical materials, which if I'm not mistaken take their roots from Eastern Philosophy. The word Karma means it is happening because maybe eons of years before your birth, certain things were planned for you and me and that nothing, can change your Karma.

Many millions of people believe that it is their Karma, or it is meant to be, or it is bershart that . . . for instance if diabetes runs in their or your family, or correctly stated . . . seems to run in your family . . . you have absolutely no control over your catching that illness. Well I'm here to state, in writing, that nothing, absolutely nothing is bershart, meant to be, or Karmic. You see, we all have been given a marvelous guide in the year of 1976, which I have been studying for the past 17 years and that guide is entitled A Course In Miracles. I remember real well when my sister Norma came to me and said, 'how come I have diabetes and you don't'? My answer to her was immediate and I remember saying 'that I choose not to buy into the belief that diabetes or heart trouble or any other ailment that seemed to run in our family, truly did. I also remember saying that 'there was no way, I would accept the worst traits that our parents and grandparents had shown us, what with all of the illnesses, diseases and even dying earlier, than necessary. I tried to explain to my kid sister Norma, that it was not being disrespectful, or in any way unloving, to not accept all of those negative, fearfilled health conditions, that so many of us, just take for granted.

The Course is one guide, one direction, one method that works, in changing our . . meant to be, our Karma, or, our bershart beliefs,

* A Course in Miracles is published by the Foundation For Inner Peace, Glen Ellen, CA.

that truly work. I've done it . . . Many people just like you have done it . . . and you can do it. Attitudinal Healing which so many people are turning to these days, most definitely works.

One of the reasons that Spirit has me writing this book is to share with you, my brothers and sisters, this most important fact that you can change your Karma, your meant to be belief, your bershart belief, simply by changing your mind. If you are a person who believes that he or she must suffer the same disasters, the same illnesses, the same so called genetic problems, the same allergies, the same negative feelings, *change your mind right now*. Even if one or both of your parents or grandparents, seemingly died too young, *change your mind today, right now*. Ask the Holy Spirit for the miracle to help you see this whole concept more clearly, so that you are not a victim of your parents or grandparents negative thinking and beliefs. Get off the belief that anything is bershart . . . meant to be . . . or Karma. You'll live longer, you'll find your health will be better, and most importantly, you'll get yourself, your spouse, and your children, into a new and far, far better belief system.

Try it . . . you'll like it.

Be Careful What You Ask For

In the movie Resurrection, there is a scene where Ellen Bursten, who has discovered that she possesses Healing abilities, is asked to go to a hospital in a nearby city to prove that she can actually heal the sick or injured. In the scene that stands out in my mind, we are taken into the hospital room of a young man, who is twisted up like a pretzel and the assumption is that this young man is inflicted with a severe case of arthritis. In the next scene we see Ms. Bursten climb into the hospital bed with the young man and after asking for Healing for this young bent over man . . . in the next scene, we see the young man completely straightened out and Ms. Bursten is then shown completely twisted up, worse than the young man had been. This memorable scene conveys two very important truths that we all need to know more about.

1. Healing Through GOD can and does take place.
2. Somehow a transference of a malady, any malady, can also take place.

I know that this whole concept is difficult to believe, but I also know that both can happen . . . since they happened to me. One evening, some years ago, Paul Steinberg, his wife Roberta, my wife Judy and I were sitting in Jerry Jampolski's living room, with Jerry and Paul for some reason known only to himself, was suffering with a rather severe infection on one of his toes. Experiencing a great deal of pain, Paul asked Jerry to help with a Healing, to help to alleviate some of the pain. As I remember, Jerry asked Paul to remove his sock and shoe on Paul's right foot and Jerry had Paul put his foot up on Jerry's knee. Jerry started to say some things from the Course and then Jerry said something to Paul that I had never heard anyone say before. Jerry's words to Paul, my cousin, my friend, my teacher, were, 'why don't you let your cousin Saul help you in your work of teaching spirituality and GOD, to everyone that Spirit sends into your life'. That remark shocked everyone in the room, most particularly, me. Feeling the need to immediately show my loyalty, my love and my allegiance, I immediately volunteered to start helping Paul immediately by volunteering to 'taking on Paul's pain. The reason being I felt at the time . . . was so that Paul could continue his most important work. That evening ended and as we all went to our respective bedrooms, I didn't think all that much about the offer I had just made, or how I was going to be of any real help to Paul.

The next morning Judy and I were scheduled to leave Tiburon, to do a book show in Los Angeles and Paul and Roberta were off to do some further touring and other lectures in another part of California. As I got out of bed and stepped down that next morning I felt a peculiar sensation on my right foot, a shooting pain, such as I had never felt before . . . and I remember thinking . . . what the hell is this? I had never experienced any thing quite like this and the pain was so severe that I could hardly walk. As I looked down at my right foot, I could see a swelling and a redness that seemed to be getting redder and more painful. When I showed my foot to Judy, the first thing she said to me was 'next time don't volunteer to take on someone elses pain'. I thought about what she said as we got into the rented car that morning and by that time the swelling of my foot was so severe that I actually had to drive without a shoe on my right foot. There was no way I could even get my foot back into my shoe and as we proceeded on our ride South towards Los Angeles, the pain and the swelling were getting worse.

Our plan was to stop the first night out at a place we had heard a great deal about, called The Madonna Inn, located in or near San Louis Obispo and from what I had heard this was considered to be one of the most unusual hotels in California with reservations needed at least one year in advance. Since I had not bothered (as usual) to make any reservations, Judy figured the one place we would not be staying at that evening, was The Madonna Inn. My foot was throbbing away and everytime I had to put my foot on the brake to slow down or stop, it was pure torture.

We finally reached The Madonna Inn and I pulled up outside of the office and when I stood in front of the girl behind the desk, I knew that if Spirit for some reason wanted me to stay at The Madonna Inn, there would be no order of difficulty. Bold as brass . . . I said to the girl that I would like a room. She looked up at me and with a half hearted smile, she asked if I had a reservation? I replied, I hadn't, but since I was a beautiful child of GOD, in whom He was well pleased, I thought there should be some room at the Inn. She didn't have the slightest idea of what I was talking about and in a rather curt tone of voice the half hearted smile completely gone from her lips she replied, 'sir at The Madonna Inn, reservations are usually made at least a full year in advance and that perhaps I should try another place down the road'.

I remembered my thoughts about Spirit and figured I'd take another shot at it and then asked the gal if she could check her cancellations and whether she had any and further to check to see whether anyone had called in on a cancellation or was arriving later than expected. She turned around and opened up a small box and I heard her say 'what do you know about this, who put this in here?' She wheeled around and said 'I just found a cancellation in the Flintstone's Suite and if you'd like to have it . . . it's yours'. I replied, I'll take it. She replied 'I haven't given you the rate yet', I replied 'I didn't ask' and I signed in and when I went back out to the car, Judy was truly astounded, when I said we had gotten the one room left at the Inn.

As we entered The Flintstone Suite, I saw why this was such a popular place. The entire room was done in huge stones and even the shower, resembled a small cave. Judy loved it, but once I carried in the luggage, the pain and throbbing of my right foot, quickly jolted me back to the reality . . that I needed a Healing. I sat down in the armchair in the corner of the room and started wondering whether or not, I had indeed bought into the illusion of Paul's pain and I wondered how a wonderful, respected teacher of GOD, as Paul surely was, could actually accept such an ego directed action. I figured out that since Paul accepted and brought in the illusion of pain, that did not mean in any way, shape or form, that I had to accept Paul's pain, or for that matter, Paul's negativity . . . or problems. All the love I could muster, all the help I could render, yes but there was clearly absolutely no need to buy into his or anyone elses pain, problems or negativity. I also finally remembered what I had seemingly forgotten on that ride from Tiburon, down to The Madonna Inn and that was . . . to ask. That's right, I was so obsessed with the pain and the swollen look of my foot, I had neglected to do the one thing, the Course and Psychotherapy says we must do . . . that is to ask Holy Spirit to help us see the whole thing differently. Go for the miracle . . . so we can open ourselves up to receive the Atonement. At that moment, I closed my eyes in prayer and asked

* A Course in Miracles and Psycotherapy, Purpose, Process and Practice are published
  by the Foundation For Inner Peace, Glen Ellen, CA.

Holy Spirit to help me to be able to see this whole episode differently. I also asked Holy Spirit to help me focus on The Light, The Perfection, and The Christ, in my cousin Paul, myself and all of my brothers and sisters everywhere on the planet.

I laid down on the bed, fell asleep and the next morning, when I awakened, the pain, the swelling, the redness, and the confusion were completely gone. Judy and I checked out of the Madonna Inn, continued our journey down to Los Angeles and had a wonderful book show.

I guess the most important lesson I personally learned from this experience, was and is . . . that you need to be most careful, as to what you volunteer for and pay extra attention to taking on anyone elses pain, problems or illnesses . . . your ego will saddle you with enough of your own, if you allow it to do so.

Beauty Is In The Eye Of The Beholder

When I was a kid growing up in the Bronx, I can remember real well . . . the feeling of revulsion, at the sight of someone who appeared to be deformed, missing a limb or even mongoloid. I always felt a funny sensation in my flow of blood, whenever I would see or be in the path of anyone, so afflicted. I guess way down deep, I considered these people in some confused way of my thinking to be different or even worse, sub-standard.

When I got involved with A Course In Miracles, I started to see things in a much different Light. I suddenly realized that the way I was seeing things became a perception and that if I wanted to hold on to this or any other perception, no one was going to stop me or even correct me . . . in my way of perceiving things.

Once reason, truth and guidance took place, I was to look at things, very much differently.

The Course says to try and look at everything through the Christ eyes, or, if that explanation isn't simple enough, to try and see the Light in everyone . . . in their true state, which is not, I repeat, not what you think you are seeing, mainly, seeing them as a body. Whether a person has three toes or one finger, or one eye, or a big nose, or any other physical characteristic, which seems to make him or her appear different, recognize that this is not the true being, you are really seeing.

The best illustration of this concept, that I can recall is an old Twilight Zone TV program I saw many years ago. The program opens with a group of surgeons, male and female, positioned around an operating table . . . diagnosing or trying to determine whether or not, they can truly offer any help to the woman lying on the operating table. All we can see of the doctors and nurses, are their hands and we hear comments on how gruesome and deformed their patient is and how a freak of nature must have given her such a grotesque appearance. All of the five or six doctors and nurses get a shot at talking about how freakish this woman appears and the revulsion that the five or six medical people seem to be feeling, leaves little to the imagination.

Slowly the camera pans over to the patient's face and we get to see what this team of medical people are so sickened by. The young

* A Course in Miracles is published by the Foundation For Inner Peace, Glen Ellen, CA.

woman on the operating table is a Marilyn Monroe look-alike, complete with the beautiful blond hair, gorgeous features and as beautiful as any Hollywood movie star. For the moment, the viewer is stunned and starts to wonder how this team of doctors and nurses could possibly find this super attractive blond bomb shell, unattractive.

Of course on the TV show they drew this episode out to last the full half hour but the gist of what was truly happening was that in this episode of Twilight Zone . . . in the last few moments of this particular episode, as the camera pans up to the faces (for the first time) of the operating team, we finally see that all of the doctors and nurses, have the faces of pigs, complete with flat noses and puffed up cheeks. We finally are allowed to figure out that somehow this freak of nature, this most beautiful woman is really a product of how we wish to see her and indeed how the operating team chooses to see her. Clearly it becomes our perception against the operating teams perception.

One of the things I have learned from my studies, of A Course In Miracles is most certainly . . . that we are not our bodies. What we see with the two eyes, located above our noses . . . is that we are not, I repeat not, seeing the true US. We are not seeing the perfect beings, we truly are. It is impossible to see the Christ . . . the perfection in our brothers and sisters, unless . . . we can see the Christ . . . the Perfection in ourselves.

The only way we can truly see the perfection in ourselves and in our brothers and sisters is through Forgiveness. Seeing the perfection in every single last one of us, regardless of who we are, what we are, whatever our physical appearance, whatever action . . . or . . . lack of action, we may have appeared to have taken . . . or . . . not taken, is for sure . . . the only way, we can see the Light, the Christ, in each other.

* A Course in Miracles is published by the Foundation For Inner Peace, Glen Ellen, CA.

My First Teacher Of A Course In Miracles

As mentioned in the dedication of this book, my first teacher of A Course In Miracles was my cousin Paul Steinberg.

Paul's thirst for knowledge began rather early, when as a young child, Paul's father and mother had a rather nasty divorce, which was to create the need for Paul to try to discover, not only the meaning of life, but also why certain events that occurred, could be happy, while other events, seemed to make us unhappy.

Paul's father Leo, came to live with our family soon after his divorce from Paul's mother Roy and Paul's search for Truth, was about to begin. At that time, Paul would spend every single weekend at our house, to be with his dad and I got to spend a great deal of time with Paul and really thought I got to know Paul real well. As I now know, I didn't really get to know Paul at all, because in his hurt, in his pain, he almost always kept up a pretense of joy, laughter and playing the clown. Inside my cousin there was really a deep seated hurt, which very few people, if any, including me, knew about and certainly were able to see. Looking back now, I really believe that I got to know the true Paul Steinberg, not in our childhood but certainly after our joint involvement with and into the Course.

Paul as I've mentioned previously, was very much aware of the existence of the Course and even though he had never read a single page of it, he was aware that he was actively searching for 'the better way' almost all of his life . . . he told me so. When we received the Course together that night in 1975, from Judy Skutch, Paul intuitively knew and predicted that the Course would become the greatest learning tool, the world had ever known. He knew and predicted early on, that there would be groups of us studying the Course, for clarification and then along with me actually started the first group. He also started and published the very first A Course In Miracles newsletter, because he knew that students everywhere, would be seeking more and more information regarding Course activities and a networking of brothers and sisters, such as the world has never seen before. He also knew that students everywhere, would want and find the need for a teaching, correspondence course, of the Course and started his facilitator's training course, based totally and entirely on A Course In Miracles. With his knowledge of

*A Course in Miracles is published by the Foundation For Inner Peace, Glen Ellen, CA.

the Course and so many other Healing Through GOD concepts that Paul had learned in his life, he was always there for anyone who asked his help in Healing Through GOD and when things were really rolling in the New York-Long Island area, Paul took off traveling all over this country, like a Johnny Appleseed and started groups, wherever he was asked to speak.

While in the army, Paul spent some time in Fort Bliss, Texas and came away with a love for that part of the country, plus a love of horses and the western culture. I can remember him going through a phase of being a Jewish cowboy from the Bronx, complete with 10 gallon hat fringed buckskin jacket and cowboy boots. Throughout all of this, Paul always kept his sense of humor and his lectures and workshops were always halted at some point, when Paul felt his audience getting too serious and he would deliver one of his great humorous stories, which would always be received with laughter, lightening the mood immediately. To some of the world he would play and appear the clown, but make no mistake about it, Paul Steinberg was, is, and has remained the earliest and best teachers of A Course In Miracles.

I never had any inkling, that Paul carried within him a deep hurt that he had been abandoned by his father, until one day at my home, he told me so. I looked at my cousin in disbelief and I found it so difficult to believe that I was hearing . . . what I was hearing. This man, this teacher of GOD, could advise the world in his very special way, that the way out of all pain was through Forgiveness and here was my cousin, seemingly not able to forgive his own father for leaving Paul's mom. As far as I know, Paul did not let go of that anger and as he started to prepare his leaving (in body) planet Earth, I noticed one more time, how his ego had somehow convinced this wonderful teacher of GOD, that he was his body. After having had his leg amputated, Judy and I visited Paul in the hospital and Paul told us that the reason that he had lost his leg was due to one of his nurses, snapping his surgical stocking, after an earlier operation to save his leg, thus rendering the operation unsuccessful. Clearly as happens to every single one of us, while we are in the body, our thinking becomes confused, unrational and we momentarily, forget who and what we truly are.

I had heard Paul, so many times tell groups of people that they

* A Course in Miracles is published by the Foundation For Inner Peace, Glen Ellen, CA.

were absolutely responsible for everything, and that meant everything, that seemed to happen to themselves, they and they alone were responsible for and here I was hearing my cousin, my teacher, my best friend, telling me that someone else . . . was responsible for Paul's 'losing' his leg. At that moment, it seemed clear to me that ego had taken over momentarily, but not for very long. After Paul's release from the hospital, he went to get himself fitted for a prosthesis and after some months he was back out on the lecture circuit, once again bringing his wisdom to all who came to listen.

As I write about my cousin Paul some six years after his decision to leave the planet, in body, as I travel all over this land of ours, I cannot deliver a talk anywhere, where I don't seem to meet someone who remembers with great love and appreciation, a humorous or serious story, shared with them by Paul. His memory is very much recorded and I'm sure in whatever annals of Truth that may exist, Paul is very prominent. I'm also certain that his search for Truth and his great spirit, will be long remembered. I'm reminded of his explanation of when and if the big dream, the illusion, will ever finally come to an end? His answer, crystal clear and always very positive and loving would always be . . . 'Yes, the world of form as we know it, will come to an end, when all of us, without exception, can see the Christ, the Light, in each and everyone of our brothers and sisters and we will practice total Unconditional Love and at that moment, everyone of us will join hands, form one giant circle, and we will all at the same time, take a mighty leap . . . and the big dream . . . the illusion . . . will at last be over, forever.

My Thoughts

GOD'S Printer . . . Me

In the late 1970's, many people were referring to me, as GOD'S Printer. The reason that I feel this was occurring, was that I had been selected to print the most successful Spiritual books of that time. First, A Course In Miracles, then Psychotherapy, Purpose, Process, Practice, followed by Louise Hay's Heal Your Body, then Jerry Fankhauser's Power Of Affirmations and hundreds more, that GOD assigned to me, one after another, after another, etc . .

The Course has taught me that there are no accidents and the more time I spend in this illusion, this big dream, the more I'm getting to believe that we all, each and everyone of us have our selected assignments and that whatever is not completed, as the introduction to the Course says, the Course is a required Course and when we do it, is up to us and there is more than enough time for us in the Grand scheme of things, to do it and that we will complete it.

The one thing that I'm certain of, is that all of the materials, I have been given to print are all, without exception, having two purposes.

1. To bring Truth, Love and Light, to as many of my brothers and sisters as the Holy Spirit, brings forward, to share this material, and
2. To Bring to myself and all of the people, who have asked me to print their books, into the special love relationships, so that we all can learn, what we're doing here and how we can turn the special love relationships, into a Holy Relationship.

I must tell you with all candor that I'm still working on the second and still have a ways to go. The answer still boils down to the simple fact, that I've been working on this number two purpose, since my introduction to the Course and thinking about it, so have the rest of us. Looking at what has been going on in my life since 1975, surely none of this is, or can be, an accident. I've learned thru all of the hundreds of books and tapes that I've printed and published that it wasn't just a matter of being at the right place at the right time, far too many things have occurred in my life to believe that. I have come to believe, that before we are born, we actually choose our mothers and fathers, somehow knowing that the parents we select are

* A Course in Miracles is published by the Foundation For Inner Peace, Glen Ellen, CA.

the two that somehow will be the correct couple to furnish us with the abilities, opportunities and even location, that we need to have, in order to do and to learn what our illusion's in life will be all about. The events and happenings in my life, truly seem to bear this whole idea out.

As a young boy growing up in the Bronx, in New York City, the one thing, as mentioned before, I constantly heard my parents arguing and fighting about was money. While my father always earned a good living, he never seemed to have enough to satisfy my mother and himself and their fights were always about their 'seeming' lack of funds. As a young boy, this eventually got to me and asking my mother for money got to be a hassle for me and I went to work with my dad at the printing plant he ran, simply to get away from the hassle of asking for money. Every day after school, I would take the subway to Manhattan, and it really felt good once a paycheck was put into my hands and I soon had enough pocket money so that I didn't have to ask or take from mom or dad. At that time I believed my issue was about money, now I know, it was about preparing for this life's work.

My father taught me his craft, and also not accidentally, it was his father's craft not accidentally, either, but that's another book. I began to wonder even then about my being a third generation printer and when I was drafted into the army during the Korean war, I was sent to Fort Knox, Kentucky, trained as a tank driver for 16 weeks and it seemed inevitable that I would be sent to Korea, to take my shot on either living or dying.

After discharge from the army, I met a wonderful gal, got married and remained in printing, moving from job to job, believing then, that the moving from job to job was about making more money. Each time I moved from job to job, what I didn't know then, but do know now is that it really had nothing to do with the money, it was again about, preparing me for this life's work.

The last job I held, while working for someone else, was the only job that I ever was discharged from, which occurred way back in 1971 over twenty years ago and at the time this happened, again I found myself wondering, was this part of 'the plan' or was it just a random happening, appearing like a leaf, just being blown from here to there and I really did wonder, what was in store for me? I was really beginning to believe that there were no accidents going on, at least not with my life. The discharge from this last job I mentioned, led me to going into my own printing and advertising business and in a very short time, I was successful enough in business to move three times in two years, each move to larger locations and still learning new avenues of communication, new technologies, new methods of reaching people and once again, further preparing me for this life's work.

In 1975 when Judith Skutch told me that I was 'selected' by Jesus and the Holy Spirit to be the printer of A Course In Miracles, my question to her at that time was . . . 'They mentioned my name?' She said yes, and again a great puzzlement was going on in my thinking. Accident, or was it part of a plan? I couldn't believe in 1975 that this was a part of a plan . . . but I believe it now. In the past eighteen years so many events have occurred with me and my special love relationships and some of the people that are in these special relationships with me are still, I believe holding on to their anger over some mistake that I've made, some mistake that they've made some mistake that we've both made and even now as I look at these events, I find no anger but there still is at least, on my part a bit of fear and try as I may, while I still send Love to these brothers and sisters, the fear is, that the Healing hasn't yet taken place. I know that it will. Again probably the most important part of my life's work, I'm still doing and will continue to do and what's in my thinking constitutes my life's work and my game plan or maybe I should say Spirit's game plan is to keep doing what I've been doing all of my life. I will continue to have my miracles and Atonements, occurring with me as I'm acting out this invisible game plan. My thoughts are that Spirit will just keep leading me down the correct road, until I get it right. That may take more than this lifetime but since we all are told, that we all have all the time we need, the sense of urgency at least for me is no longer a concern.

Tomorrow, the Holy Spirit has arranged for me to see a lady in Naples that I met several years ago and at that time she was on her journey and not by accident, coming out of her bout with terminal cancer. She and I spoke and she purchased our cancer tape and some books and now several years later has invited me to drive across Alligator Alley and talk to her about bringing her story about beating

---

* A Course in Miracles is published by the Foundation For Inner Peace, Glen Ellen, CA.

cancer to our brothers and sisters, so they can learn what she, I and a great many other brothers and sisters have learned, that we don't have to be sick and that we don't even have to die. Accident, or part of our mutual life's work? I am certain it's no accident.

My role as GOD'S Printer seems to be ongoing and I can only tell you that at this time in my life, I would not change places with anyone and I mean anyone. My life's work has filled my days, my nights, my time spent with my family of brothers and sisters with so much love and joy, that I find myself these days, leaping out of bed at five thirty in the morning, every morning, to get the new day underway and learn what Spirit has planned for me, for today's 'Life's Work'. As the song says . . . The Best Is Yet To Come . . . for GOD'S Printer.

Nothing Real Can Be Threatened
Nothing Unreal Exists
Herein lies the peace of God

The above are the last three lines of the introduction of A Course In Miracles and most likely, the most meaningful words in the entire Course. It has taken me a long time to understand the meaning of these words and I think that now, eighteen years after setting the type, printing and binding, the fears I used to live with are all gone. All of the so-called problems I used to live with, are no longer problems at all, they're long gone. The nothing real can be threatened part, is so true. As I look back at all the events, the authors I've had sent to me, the books, we produced, the hundreds of tapes, etc., I am now most definitely beginning to believe that all of the mistakes, I made, the mistakes, they made, that we jointly made, were made for our mutual learning. The anger, the frustration, the disagreements, even the legal threats, were all part of our joint learning experience, to demonstrate, to all of us, that 'nothing real can be threatened'. I believe I finally understand that line at this time and that no matter what seems to be happening, no matter how severe the disappointment, or the disagreement, appears to be, at the time, what we need to do, is Love, Forgive and believe that, **'nothing real can be threatened'.** You see the **'nothing real'** is everything that is of GOD, everything that's permanent and that, brothers and sisters, includes you and me.

'Nothing Unreal Exists'

Here's another gem of Truth and Wisdom. So many of us have such a big problem believing this lovely teaching, which is the Truth, that the illusion, the big dream, as we are calling it, is not real and most definitely is just that, a big dream, an illusion. Our desire to make the illusion real, is the most difficult one that most people I meet, have the most trouble with. Believing that none of this stuff that we deal with on a day to day basis, truly is happening at all, is a tough one to believe. At my lectures, I usually wait till the end of my talks, to inform my brothers and sisters who have come to meet me and hear me, that GOD did not create the world of form, that we did. Most people, me included, were of the belief that GOD created

* A Course in Miracles is published by the Foundation For Inner Peace, Glen Ellen, CA.

everything that we see with the two eyes above our noses, but according to the Course, none of these things were created by GOD, but are also a part of the illusion. It's what we can't see with our two eyes, that is truly of GOD, such as GOD Herself/Himself and the True Us . . . The Spirit Us.

When we look at anything using our Christ eyes, which every single one of us have, once we believe we truly have them, we are then able to look past the world of form and see precisely what GOD has truly created and that again means you and me. GOD created the Real, the Permanent, the Loving. All of the rest is nothing, just a great big fat dream, not even truly existing. I really don't know how many of my brothers and sisters walk out of my talks, believing a word I've said but I do know that the hugs, the smiles, the joy and most importantly, the Love just flows, like I've never seen it flow before. A new consciousness is there, that didn't seem to be there before.

'Herein lies the peace of GOD.'

I'm convinced at this point in my life that what each and everyone of us has entered into the illusion to search for, is the thing we never lost, that thing is, the Peace of GOD. Notice I say we've never really lost that Peace of GOD but so many of us spend our lives frantically searching and in most cases, we don't even know we're searching for something we've never truly lost. Without a doubt, the Peace of GOD is the most exquisite feeling, anyone can experience. It means that there is no fear, no guilt, no illness, no depression, no pain, no suffering, no anger, no deprivation, no crisis, no loss, no sadness, no doubt and most assuredly, no unhappiness.

Knowing the Peace of GOD fills your very being with Joy, with Laughter, with Abundance, with Happiness, with Truth, with Sharing, with Christ, with Spirit, with Revelation, with Vision, with Salvation, with Belief, with Knowledge and most assuredly, the Will of GOD.

The Peace of GOD is a happiness, beyond what can be felt, the Peace of GOD is a feeling beyond what can be compared to anything else, and the Peace of GOD, is a way of living . . . never before experienced. I wish to end this book, the very same way I began it, by reminding you, once again, that . . .

You . . . are a beautiful child
of a Loving Mother/Father GOD,
In whom He/She is well pleased.

Saul Steinberg considers himself to be
first, a teacher of GOD,
second, a Loving brother,
and third, a lecturer, a businessman and an author.
He now resides permanently in Fort Lauderdale, Florida
and is available to speak at your facility
and can be reached at:

Saul Steinberg
16363 Cammi Lane
Fort Lauderdale, Florida 33326
305-389-8076

Much Love and Many Thanks

Saul Steinberg has now completed more
than 1,000 Books, Audios, and Videos
and any of his materials are available
from:

Mind and Miracles
16363 Cammi Lane
Ft. Lauderdale, Florida 33326
305-389-8076